ALSO BY HASSE BUNNELLE

Food for Knapsackers
(with Winnie Thomas)

Cooking for Camp and Trail
(with Shirley Sarvis)

The Backpacker's Food Book

by Hasse Bunnelle

and the Editors
of *Backpacker* Magazine

A Fireside Book
Published by Simon and Schuster
NEW YORK

Published by Simon and Schuster
A Division of Gulf & Western Corporation
Simon & Schuster Building
Rockefeller Center
1230 Avenue of the Americas
New York, New York 10020
SIMON AND SCHUSTER and colophon are trademarks of Simon & Schuster
FIRESIDE and colophon are trademarks of Simon & Schuster
Portions of the work have previously appeared in Backpacker Magazine.

Designed by Elizabeth Woll
Manufactured in the United States of America

Pbk.   10   9   8   7   6   5   4   3   2   1

Library of Congress Cataloging in Publication Data

Bunnelle, Hasse.
    The backpacker's food book.

    (A Fireside book)
    Bibliography: p.
    Includes index.
    1. Outdoor cookery. 2. Backpacking. I. Backpacker.
II. Title.
TX823.B853   641.5′78   80–12478
ISBN 0–671–25032–9

ACKNOWLEDGMENTS

For the backpacker, food is the fuel necessary to keep going. It provides the energy we use. The weight of fuel, for man or machine, is the weight of life. We are not machines to gulp gasoline, but people who can enjoy what we eat; who make of eating an aesthetic pleasure to enhance the camps we find, the skies we see at dawn and sunset, the snow on ridges, sunlit slopes among hillside trees, swift streams, and all weathers. Fast or slow, in preparation and in eating, food celebrates the magic of living, makes the magic brighter. Food is both fuel and grace. The best is planned and prepared with simplicity, ease, and imagination.

I am grateful for the goodwill, generosity, and imagination of those backpackers and other friends who contributed recipes for this book: Wesley P. Bunnelle, Nancy Chilton, Peter Graham, Margo Gwinn, Paul Friedman, Roxanne Friedman, Carol Flato, Isabelle Kroger, Jerrold Kluchin, Betty Pillsbury, and Luella K. Sawyer.

I am grateful, too, for the help of William Kemsley, Jr., and the editors of *Backpacker Magazine,* and to all of our readers who shared with us their experiences in the kitchen and on the trail, to make possible the *Movable Feasts* column and this cookbook. To all: May we share better meals, lighter packs, and many more miles on the trails.

HASSE RUSSELL BUNNELLE

Contents

Backpacker Basics

MENU PLANNING

Food is the fuel on which we travel, but eating need not be a fast-fuel stop, even on the hiking trail. Whatever we eat should be nutritious, colorful, fragrant, and flavorful. Food is an important part of any outing; it need not be difficult to prepare.

The content of the menu depends on the time of year—winter, summer, snow or desert; the length of the trip—one day or several weeks; high or low elevations; and pace—strenuous or leisurely. Is the trip designed to set a mileage record, or to enjoy the scenery, watch and photograph wildlife and plants? How many people, and what are their approximate ages and sizes? Younger and older people usually eat less, but this is not always true. Some hikers past seventy have legs as hollow as boys of seventeen. A teenage boy or girl may be counted, for menu purposes, as one-and-a-half or two adults. Know the party and its fueling requirements.

To simplify planning, lay out a chart: number of days, meals served each day, then list the foods to take along. Consider the keeping quality, weight, and nutritional components. For a one-day outing, or for a weekend, fresh and frozen foods may be used. A first night's dinner for a longer trip can be fresh food. Solid-pack cans of meat are more useful than cans of food with a high water content. Dried foods are good for the longer trip, and may be prepared at home, packaged and ready to eat in camp or on the trail.

It is possible to do little or no cooking and still eat well. Plan the menus and recipes, prepare the items, package and label each for the planned day and meal. Toss in a surprise or two for those days when the going may be hard, when an extra bit of color, flavor, or fragrance may be needed to cheer the day.

Flexibility is the key to good planning. The menu should be variable to suit weather, changes in plans, or changes of mind for any reason, to make the trip more comfortable, more enjoyable, more adventurous, if that is what the party wants.

Take weather into consideration. Make it part of the enjoyment —the adventure—of the outing. Foods that need no cooking, that may be eaten at any time, come into focus on the day the stove fails to work, or if there is no stove on the outing. If the trip is in a desert where little water is available, plan meals that need little or no water to prepare.

Take care to avoid taking along too much food, but do plan for emergencies—a day's delay, an extra-cold day when more calories are needed. This is a safety factor, and the food is not wasted even if it must be carried out, uneaten. Extra soup and bouillon cubes often fill the need for emergency rations. Nuts, chocolate, fruit and nut breads, are good extras.

Don't refrain from seasoning food for the dubious reason that "people don't like" seasoned foods. While highly spiced or exceptionally fat foods are not desirable at high elevations, there are times and places for such meals. Many flavorful herbs, items such as ginger root and garlic, may be used to add zest to freeze-dried or dehydrated meals. Don't use the same seasoning in every dish, or mix too many flavors into one meal. Preparation of food is an art. Seasoning is part of the art and should be done with care, flair, and consideration of all the senses. It is not necessary to spend extra time; planning ahead is the answer.

SAMPLE MENUS

This assortment of sample daily menus contains enough protein for active people. *Many menus contain fresh foods useful for first and second days only, or for weekends.* Such items could be replaced with dried meats, cheeses, or other foods. Provide at least 65 grams of protein per person per day, with sufficient carbohydrates and fat to fill and satisfy all appetites.

BREAKFAST	LUNCH	DINNER
Creamed Chipped Soup	Charqui con Chile	Mizu Taki w/Sprouts
Pilot Bread	Granola, Fruit	Chocolate Bombers
Instant Applesauce	Milk	Tea w/Lemon Drops
Coffee, Milk		
Instant Fruit Juice	Cheese, Crackers	Chicken and
Trail Eggs	Trail Mix	Dumplings
Coffee, Tea	Chocolate Bars	Carrot, Celery Sticks
		Mincemeat Bars
		Coffee, Cocoa

BREAKFAST	LUNCH	DINNER
Sour Cream Foldovers with Strawberries	Cheese Balls w/Nut Bread	Lentils with Lamb
Cheese	Salami	Fruitcake
Barley Coffee	Aplets	Herb Tea
	Lemonade	
Grape-Nuts, Milk	Sardines with Rye Bread	Vegetable Soup
Cottage Cheese w/Dates, Figs, or Berries	Green Onions	Meat Loaf
Coffee, Tea	Fruit Balls	Bannock w/Stewed Apples and Figs
	Lemonade or Tea	Herb Tea, Coffee
Fruit Juice	Pita, Cream Cheese, Olives, Alfalfa Sprouts	Vegetable Soup
Whole Wheat Muffins	Trail Mix, Applesauce	Grilled Trout
Omelet w/Bacon Bits	Lemonade, Tea	Green Rice with Mushrooms
Coffee or Tea		(Add chopped ham if no trout caught)
		Spiced Fruit
		Mocha
Sun Cloud Granola, Milk	Sushi with Pickled Herring	Mongolian Fire Pot
Omelet with Guacamole	Boiled Eggs	Fruitcake
Tea, Cocoa, Coffee	Persimmon Bread	Tea
	Iced Tea	
Instant Applesauce	Apricot Nut Bread	Chicken Noodle Soup
Rice and Raisin Cereal	Jerky, Cheddar Cheese	Navajo Taco
Freeze-dried Sausage	Lemonade	Spinach Salad
Coffee, Tea		Carob Fudge
		Coffee
Instant Freeze-dried Scrambled Eggs with Grated Cheese, or Alfalfa Sprouts	Salami, Crackers	Split-Pea Soup
Fresno Bran Muffins with Butter	Honey Quick Bread and Cheese	Walnut-Oat Patties w/Cashew Sauce
Orange Juice	Tea, Milk, or Lemonade	Stewed Fruit Compote with Peppermint Topping
Coffee, Tea, Cocoa		Tea, Coffee, Cocoa

Whether it is the golden trout of the Sierra Nevada, the rainbow, or the brown, nothing is as delicious in camp as delicately flavored fresh trout. It needs little seasoning.

Fry-pan Bread with
   Berries
Trout and Herbs
Coffee, Tea

Cold Boned Trout
   Rolled in a
     Tortilla or Pita
Alfalfa Sprouts
Cheese
Mountain Bars
Lemonade

Trout Chowder
Berries or
   Spiced Stewed Fruit
Hot Chocolate or
   Mocha

SEASONINGS: *Herbs, Spices, and Seeds*

Fresh herbs may be carried in plastic bags and are superior in flavor and fragrance to dried herbs. If fresh herbs are not available, use the freshest dry herbs in leaf form. Ground herbs are usually too old and bitter to provide good seasoning. Store the leaves, seeds, or ground spices in 35mm. film cans, labeled, and take along to add to eggs, soups, stews, rice or other grains, or noodles for color, flavor, and fragrance.

ALLSPICE: Resembles other spices and may be used in the same way as cinnamon, nutmeg, cloves, or mace.

ANISE SEED: Licorice-flavored seeds. Good in breads, cookies, candies, or with raw or cooked carrots.

BASIL LEAVES: Plants may be grown at home, bought fresh in Italian markets, or in dried form on grocery shelves. Use in tomato dishes, green vegetables, fish, and meats—particularly with lamb.

BAY LEAVES: Leaves of the laurel tree. Use sparingly in stews, soups, tomato dishes, and for pickling.

CARAWAY SEED: Fruit of a plant grown in Europe, and widely used in baking, sauerkraut, noodles, cheese, meats, fried potatoes, or breads.

CARDAMOM SEEDS: The seed may be bought ground or whole; used in pickling, Mexican dishes, pastries, Middle Eastern dishes, or as a breath sweetener.

CAYENNE: Hot peppers used in meats, soups, stews, sauces, eggs. Add to butter for cooked vegetables.

CELERY SEED: Use in pickles, salads, vegetables, dressings, cheeses, or in breads and crackers, fish or potatoes.

CHERVIL LEAVES: Resembles parsley in flavor. Good in soups, salads, eggs, fish, chicken, and vegetables—particularly spinach.

CHIVES: A member of the onion family. Used in salads, vegetables, cottage cheese, eggs, potatoes, or dressings.

CHIA SEEDS: A small black seed from a mustardlike plant used by Southwestern American Indians. Dried seeds are rich in oil, were made into flour or toasted as a snack while traveling. Use in cereals, trail snacks, breads.

CHILI POWDER: A blend of chile peppers and other spices. Use to season eggs, stews, corn dishes, ground meats, and fish.

CINNAMON (CASSIA): Bark of cinnamon tree or a similar tree which provides cassia buds and bark, with a cinnamonlike flavor. Much cinnamon is really cassia. Use in fruit mixtures, baking, chocolate recipes, pickles, and preserves.

CLOVES: Bud of clove tree. Use in baked foods, puddings, stews, fruits, desserts, pickles, and preserves.

CORIANDER SEED AND LEAF: Used ground in baking, stuffings, sausages, meats, curries. Green leaves are called "Chinese parsley" or "cilantro" and have a pleasant, unique flavor in salads, vegetables, soups, rice, or as garnishes.

CUMIN SEED (COMINO): Used in curry powder, chili powder, and other mixtures of spices. Use in soups, cheeses, fruit mixtures, pies, chutney, chilis, and other Mexican foods. Good in corn dishes.

CURRY POWDER: Mixture of peppers and spices for curried foods, salad dressings, fish dishes, soups, eggs, rice, and bulgur.

DILL SEED AND WEED: Used in pickles, sauerkraut, salads, beans, beet soups, fish, pies, potatoes, pastas. A stalk of dill in a bottle of vinegar makes dill vinegar. Use in many ways, in cottage cheese and yoghurt.

FENNEL SEED, LEAVES, BULBS: Similar in flavor to anise. Use seeds in pickles, fish, baked foods, candies, liqueurs, pies. Leaves flavor sauces, salads, spaghetti; bulbs may be eaten as a vegetable—steamed, or as a salad.

FENUGREEK SEED: Member of pea family. The seed is used ground in curry powder. The whole seed sprouts well, or may be used as a fragrant and delicious tea.

GARLIC CLOVES, POWDER: Use the cloves—dried, fresh, or cooked—or powder in soups, stews, salad dressings, eggs, meats, breads, or roasted with meats and vegetables. The cooked flavor is milder.

GINGER ROOT, GROUND, CANDIED: Ginger root may be grated or minced in fruit mixtures, meats, salads, pastas, fruit drinks, Oriental dishes. Ground ginger is used in baked foods, fruits, fish, and meat dishes. Use candied (crystallized) ginger in fruitcakes, desserts.

HORSERADISH: Related to mustard, the root is hot and pungent. Comes prepared in vinegar, or dried, and is good with meats, salad dressings, sour cream sauce, or as a relish. Add it last when it is used in cooking soups and stews.

MACE: Lining between nutmeg shell and husk. Used in baked foods, fruit mixtures, pickles, and breads. Adds delicate flavor in whipped cream, sauces.

MARJORAM LEAVES: Member of mint family. Use in stews, soups, meats, fish, and sauces, cooked vegetables, omelets, or poultry dishes. Use with thyme, or alone.

MINT LEAVES: There are several varieties of mint. Use it fresh in drinks, fruit dishes, cottage cheese, tabbouli, or lamb. Use dried in lamb dishes, with peas, carrots, desserts.

MUSTARD SEED, GROUND: Seeds are used in pickles, potatoes, pastas, and in baking. Dry mustard is used in stews, sauces, dressings, pickles and fish dishes. Prepared mustards are made with ground mustard and other spices, oils, vinegars.

NUTMEG, WHOLE, GROUND: Fruit of nutmeg plant, it is used ground in baked foods, sauces, vegetables, and other foods in which other spices may be used. May be bought whole and ground fresh.

OREGANO LEAVES: Member of sage family. Use in meats, beans, tomato sauces, eggs, Mexican foods. Stronger than marjoram but similar in flavor.

PAPRIKA: A sweet capsicum (pepper). Use in fish, salad dressings, vegetables, cheeses, meats. Flavor is mild; red color is valuable, particularly in sauces.

PARSLEY: Fresh parsley may be used in soups, vegetables, stews, as a garnish, or taken along frozen or dried. Use dried parsley in meats, stews, soups, salads, fish, vegetables, sauces.

PEPPER, BLACK: Dried berries of a vine. White pepper is black peppercorn with outer cover removed. Used in almost every kind of food for additional flavor.

POPPY SEED: Seeds of poppy plant are the smallest used in our foods. Good in breads, cookies, vegetables, meats, salads, rice, pastas, and particularly in pastries.

ROSEMARY LEAVES: A fragrant herb that looks like a pine needle. Use sparingly, as it is strong, in soups, tomato dishes, meats, fish, potatoes, Italian dishes. Good also as a hot tea, a hair rinse, a fragrant herb to burn.

SAGE: A pungent herb used with pork dishes, stuffings, fish, poultry, salads, or soups. Also makes a good hot tea, a fragrant herb to burn.

SAFFRON: The stigma of a crocus, it is used to color foods yellow, to season sauces, fish, poultry, rice, baked foods.

SAVORY LEAVES: A mild-flavored member of the mint family used in meats, dressings, sauces, stuffings, eggs, alone or combined with other herbs.

SESAME SEEDS: Small sweetish seeds also called benne seeds. Used in baking, fruit mixtures, granola, vegetables, and candies.

SHALLOTS: A mild member of the onion family, used in any way onions or garlic may be used as a seasoning.

TARRAGON LEAVES: A flavorful leaf used in sauces, soups, salad dressings, tomato dishes, eggs, meats, cottage cheese. Very good with fish or fowl.

SWEET MARJORAM: A member of the mint family, used in fish, eggs, soups, sauces, salad dressings, vegetables, and meats—particularly lamb.

THYME LEAVES: There are several thymes, including lemon thyme. Good in soups, stews, poultry dishes, tomatoes, salad dressings, eggs, sausages, creamed dishes.

TURMERIC: A root of the ginger family, used mostly for its yellow color in pickles, curry powders, fish, rice, pastas.

VANILLA: Vanilla beans are used to flavor hot milk, coffee, cocoa, other hot drinks. The extract is a sweet flavoring for baked goods, candies, desserts.

SOY SAUCE (SHOYU): Made of soybeans and wheat by fermentation, it is highly salty. One of the ingredients of Worcestershire sauce. Use in eggs, Oriental dishes, to marinate meats and fish, in salad dressings. When using soy sauce, do not add salt.

FREEZE-DRIED, DEHYDRATED AND OTHER CONVENIENCE FOODS

Freeze-dried foods will continue to be more expensive than fresh or home-dried foods. The special vacuum process is expensive, and the foods are prepared for a special purpose: lighter weight in the pack, longer shelf- and/or pack-life. For trips of only a few days' duration, freeze-dried foods usually are not practical. For those who have neither time nor inclination to prepare dried foods at home, or for those who plan trips of a week or longer, the convenience outweighs the cost factor.

Dehydrated foods are less expensive, but weigh more than freeze-dried items, since drying does not remove all water—particularly from fruits.

The dried-food market is fairly competitive. Manufacturers do make an effort to learn and to satisfy the needs and wants of the backpacker. Most products on the market are satisfactory; some items are superior—particularly fruits. Choice is largely a matter of taste, but a few rules should govern choices:

• Avoid any food in which the major component is sugar. It is cheaper to buy foods without sugar, or with a minimum. Extra sugar is best provided at home or in camp, to individual taste and dietary needs.
• Avoid excessive salt. Salt is also cheaper to add at home, or in camp, to suit individual taste and dietary needs.
• Choose foods with a minimum of packaging. Avoid packages in which the foil, plastic, or paper equals the food in weight and volume.
• Preservatives are necessary in the preparation of most freeze-dried and dehydrated foods, and other processed foods. Become familiar with the chemicals used and listed on the packages. Buy those using fewest, least dangerous chemicals. This is not easy, but the more aware the consumer, the more aware the manufacturer will be of consumer desires.
• Large sizes are cheaper and more efficient to buy *if* home storage space permits, and if the product won't be kept longer than a year.
• In addition to mountaineering supply stores, supermarkets, Oriental and other ethnic food stores, specialty shops, surplus, and damaged merchandise outlets, provide good buys in dried or canned foods.

Some suppliers of freeze-dried foods are:
CAMPLITE: Perma-Pak, 40 East 2430 South, Salt Lake City, Utah 84115
CHUCK WAGON: Micro Drive, Woburn, Massachusetts 01801
DRI-LITE: 11333 Atlantic Avenue, Lynwood, California 90262
HARDEE: in equipment stores in Canada, or order from Freeze-Dry Foods Limited, 579 Speers Road, Oakville, Ontario, Canada L6K 2G4
MARSHALL: Marshall Produce Company, P.O. Box 1088, Marshall, Minnesota 56258

MOUNTAIN HOUSE: in equipment stores, through many mail-order equipment suppliers or through Stow-Lite (below). Catalog available from Oregon Freeze Dry Foods, Box 1048, Albany, Oregon 97321

RICH-MOOR: in equipment stores or through mail-order firms. Catalog available from Rich-Moor Corporation, Box 2728, Van Nuys, California 91404

SEIDEL'S: National Packaged Trail Foods, 18607 St. Clair Avenue, Cleveland, Ohio 44110

STOW-LITE: Stow-a-Way Sports Industries, 166 Cushing Highway (Route 3A), Cohasset, Massachusetts 02025

WILSON'S: in equipment stores, through mail-order firms or through Rich-Moor

Suppliers of cheeses, salamis, sprouts, and other foods are:

HICKORY FARMS OF OHIO: stores in most major cities, suburban shopping centers

SPROUT PACK DIVISION: 2145 Everding Street, Eureka, California 95501, mail order, or in equipment stores

FOOD VALUES

PROTEIN

Protein comes from a Greek word meaning "of first place." Proteins are made up of chains of amino acids, lysine, and methionine, that contain nitrogen, which is essential to life. Some amino acids can be created from reserves of fat, sugar, and the nitrogen freed from the breakdown of used protein. The eight amino acids which cannot be synthesized are called essential amino acids. Foods such as egg yolks (6 grams of protein each), milk (8 oz. whole milk = 8 grams), cheese (4 oz. cottage cheese = 22 grams), and a slice of lean beef (4" x 3" x 1" = 20 grams) are rich in usable protein. All animal protein except egg white and gelatin is complete. Soybeans, brewer's yeast, and wheat germ are also complete proteins. Most vegetable protein is incomplete but is valuable nevertheless.

The average American adult consumes 100 to 110 grams of protein daily—almost twice the amount needed, except for great activity. The excess is not needed to build blood, enzymes, hormones, and tissues, and is stored in the body as fat. The nitrogen portion of the protein is excreted in the urine.

CARBOHYDRATES

Carbohydrates are organic compounds consisting of carbon, hydrogen, and oxygen—sugars, starches, cellulose—which break down into simple sugars in the digestive process. Cellulose provides fiber. Carbohydrates provide from 45 percent to 90 percent of the daily energy intake. Highly developed countries use less; the less developed countries use more. Unneeded carbohydrates are stored in the body as fat. Almost all foods contain carbohydrates.

CALORIES

A calorie is a unit of energy utilized by the human body. One hundred calories is the approximate equivalent of: 1 banana, 20 stalks of celery, 1 oz. blue cheese, one-fourth cup corned beef hash, 1 slice of French bread, 2 chocolate chip cookies, 80 radishes, 1 cup unsweetened applesauce, 1 pear, one-fifth honeydew melon, 3 oz. canned shrimp, or 4 oz. table wine. One cup of hulled sunflower seeds equals 800 calories.

VITAMINS

Vitamins are life-giving organic substances found in all food which are necessary for the body to survive in health. Recommended Daily Allowances approved by the Food and Drug Administration as nutritional guides are:

VITAMIN A: 5,000 units. Good sources are fish, liver, eggs, butter, yellow vegetables, spinach, turnips, beet greens, carrots, sweet potatoes, and tomatoes. Fat-soluble Vitamin A is destroyed by overcooking.

VITAMIN B-1 (*Thiamine*): 1.5 milligrams. Sources are rice, bran, soy flour, mushrooms, turkey, nuts, liver, lentils, dried beans.

VITAMIN B-2 (*Riboflavin*): 1.7 milligrams. Sources are yeast, kidneys, avocados, wheat germ, bran, whole grains, green leafy vegetables. Destroyed by sunlight and cooking.

VITAMIN B-6 (*Pyridoxine*): 2 milligrams. Sources are beef, pork, liver, kidneys, heart, molasses, wheat germ, milk, eggs, cabbage, and beets. Destroyed by cooking and long storage.

VITAMIN B-12 (*Cyanocobalamin*): 3 micrograms. Sources are liver, kidneys, milk, eggs, cheese, and most meats. Strict vegetarians may develop B-12 anemia over a period of years. Resistant to heat, but destroyed by sunlight, acids, and alkalis.

OTHER MEMBERS OF THE B-COMPLEX:

Biotin: 150–300 micrograms. Synthesized in the body. Found in yeast, egg yolk, milk, liver.

Choline: No RDA established. Found in brains, liver, kidneys, wheat germ, brewer's yeast, egg yolk. Part of structure of lecithin, a common constituent of animal and plant tissues.

Folic acid (Folacin): 0.4 milligrams; perhaps more is necessary. Found in liver, kidneys, green vegetables, nuts, cereals, fruits. Cooking causes loss.

Inositol: No RDA established. Found in liver, brewer's yeast, wheat germ, whole grains, oatmeal, corn, unrefined molasses. Part of structure of lecithin.

Niacin (Nicotinic acid): 18–20 milligrams; perhaps more. Found in brewer's yeast, liver, kidneys, wheat germ, whole grains, fish, eggs, lean meats, beans, peas, peanuts. Resists heat, but is leached out in cooking water. Deficiency leads to pellagra.

Pantothenic acid: No RDA established; perhaps 10–30 milligrams. Found in liver, kidneys, heart, wheat germ, bran, green vegetables, brewer's yeast. Easily destroyed in canning and overcooking. Deficiencies have been associated with hypoglycemia.

Para-amino benzoic acid (PABA): Up to 30 milligrams. Found in liver, kidneys, whole grains, brewer's yeast, foods rich in other B-complex vitamins.

Bioflavonoids (once called Vitamin P): No RDA established. Plant substances that affect strength of blood vessel walls. Found in fruit pulps, currants, rose hips, asparagus, apricots. Destroyed by boiling and air.

VITAMIN C (*Ascorbic acid*): 45 milligrams for adults, more for infants and children. Found in all fresh foods, citrus fruits, guavas, bell peppers, rose hips, tomato juice, strawberries, cabbage. Plays a vital role in the immunity system. Easily lost in heat and air. Is neither stored in the body nor synthesized. Said to protect body proteins from changes brought about by near ultraviolet rays. Smokers seem to need it in larger quantities than do other adults.

VITAMIN D (*Calciferol*): 400 I.U. Found in fish-liver oils, milk fortified with Vitamin D, eggs, cheese, butter, sunlight on the oils of the skin. Is fat soluble. May be toxic in large quantities—2,000 I.U. or more.

VITAMIN E (*Tocopherol*): 15 I.U. for adults; more may be necessary. Found in unrefined vegetable oils, wheat germ, whole grains, nuts, eggs, peas and beans, fresh greens. Fat soluble, it is destroyed by heating, freezing, storage, exposure to air.

VITAMIN K: No RDA established. Found in green vegetables; synthesized in intestines. Fat soluble, as are A, D, and E. Deficiency is rare.

MINERALS

Minerals are inorganic substances needed by the body to grow and function properly. RDA has been established for some, but more may be necessary, depending on individual metabolism and needs.

CALCIUM: 1 gram. Needed for bones and teeth. Milk and milk products, soybeans, greens, are good sources. Absorption depends on Vitamin D.

MAGNESIUM: 300–400 milligrams. Interdependent with Vitamin B-6. Found in most vegetables. Whole grains, soybeans, nuts. green leaves, are good sources. Lost in boiled vegetables.

PHOSPHORUS: Found in body in 1 to 1.5 ratio with calcium. Found in calcium-rich foods.

POTASSIUM: No RDA established; perhaps 1 gram. Found in vegetables, fruits, grains, meats, nuts. Helps sodium maintain balance of fluids in cells and helps phosphorus carry oxygen to brain cells.

SODIUM: No RDA established; perhaps 1 gram. Found in most foods, and in great amounts in processed foods. Excessive sodium intake causes potassium loss.

TRACE ELEMENTS: Minerals required in very small amounts are bromide, chromium, cobalt, copper, fluoride, iodine, manganese, molybdenum, and zinc. Found in leafy vegetables, whole grains, seafood, liver, kidneys, and other foods, usually in sufficient quantities. Iodine may be missing due to lack in some soils. Other nutrients may be missing from overused soils, but there are divergent views on the matter, and the subject will require greater study.

Some food values of commonly used camp and trail food items, taken from U.S. Department of Agriculture listings.

FOOD ITEM	Amount	Grams	Calories	Protein Grams	Carbohydrate Grams	Sodium Mg.
MILK AND MILK PRODUCTS						
Milk, whole, cow's	8 oz.	244	160	8.5	11.9	122
Buttermilk	8 oz.	244	88	8.8	12.4	317
Milk, skimmed	8 oz.	244	88	8.8	12.5	128
Milk, evaporated	4 oz.	126	173	8.8	12.2	149
Milk, dry, whole	1 Tbsp.	7	35	1.8	2.7	28
Milk, dry, nonfat	1 Tbsp.	7	25	2.5	3.6	37
Milk, goat's	8 oz.	244	163	7.8	11.2	83
Sour cream	2 Tbsp.	30	57	0.8	1.0	12
Cream substitute, dry	1 tsp.	2	10	0.2	1.2	N/A
Sour cream, imitation, dry	8 oz.	235	440			
Cheese, Cheddar	1 oz.	28	113	7.1	0.6	198
Cheese, cottage, creamed	⅓ cup	75	80	10.2	2.2	172
Cheese, cottage, uncreamed	⅓ cup	75	65	12.7	2.0	218

N/A—Not available.
N/D—Not determined.

FOOD ITEM	Amount	Grams	Calories	Protein Grams	Carbohydrate Grams	Sodium Mg.
Cheese, cream	1 oz.	28	106	2.3	0.6	71
Parmesan	1 oz.	28	111	10.2	0.8	208
Roquefort	1 oz.	28	104	6.1	0.6	
Swiss, natural	1 oz.	28	105	7.8	0.5	201
Yoghurt, skimmed milk	8 oz.	244	123	8.4	12.8	125
MEATS, POULTRY, FISH						
Beef, ground, broiled	4 oz.	114	326	27.6	0	68
Beef, chuck, boneless, lean	4 oz.	114	220	34.7	0	68
Beef, sirloin, bone in	4 oz.	114	236	36.7	0	68
Beef, corned, canned	4 oz.	114	246	28.8	0	1,000 (approx.)
Beef, dried, chipped	4 oz.	114	231	39.1	0	1,565
Beef, roast, canned	4 oz.	114	334	14.8	0	N/D
Liverwurst	4 oz.	114	350	18.5	2.0	N/D
Salami, dry	4 oz.	114	513	27.1	1.4	N/D
Lamb, broiled, lean, bone in	4.8 oz.	136	140	20.8	0	52

N/A—Not available.
N/D—Not determined.

FOOD ITEM	Amount	Grams	Calories	Protein Grams	Carbohydrate Grams	Sodium Mg.
Bacon, fried	4 oz.	114	696	34.6	3.6	1,164
Bacon, Canadian, fried	1 oz.	21	58	5.8	trace	536
Ham, boiled	4 oz.	114	266	21.6	0	N/D
Ham, canned, deviled	2 oz.	57	200	7.8	0	N/D
Sausages, smoked	4 oz.	114	393	17.2	0	N/D
Sausages, Vienna	4 oz.	114	274	16.0	0.3	N/D
Sausages, frankfurter	2 oz.	51	151	6.7	1.3	N/D
Sausages, scrapple	4 oz.	114	245	10.0	16.6	N/D
Chicken, broiled, boneless	4 oz.	114	155	27.1	0	75
Chicken, canned	4 oz.	114	226	24.7	0	N/D
Turkey, dark, roasted	4 oz.	114	232	34.3	0	113
Turkey, light, roasted	4 oz.	114	201	37.6	0	94
Turkey, canned, boned	4 oz.	114	231	23.9	0	N/D
Clams, canned	4 oz.	114	112	18.0	2.2	N/D
Herring, pickled	2 oz.	57	127	11.6	0	699

N/A—Not available.
N/D—Not determined.

FOOD ITEM	Amount	Grams	Calories	Protein Grams	Carbohydrate Grams	Sodium Mg.
Lobsters, canned	8 oz.	227	216	42.4	0.7	477
Oysters, canned	4 oz.	114	87	9.7	5.6	N/D
Sardines, canned	3 oz.	85	173	20.4	0	699
Shrimp, canned	3 oz.	85	99	20.6	0.6	N/D
Salmon, canned	4 oz.	114	195	23.2	0	596
Salmon, smoked	2 oz.	57	100	12.3	0	N/D
MEAT ALTERNATIVES						
Eggs, large	1	50	81	6.4	0.4	61
Beans, pinto, calico, red, dry	4 oz.	114	396	26.1	72.6	11
Beans, garbanzos (chickpeas), dry	4 oz.	100	360	20.5	61.0	26
Lentils, dry	4 oz.	110	374	27.1	66.1	33
Peas, black-eyed (cowpeas), boiled	½ cup	80	86	6.5	14.5	1
Bean, limas, boiled	½ cup	80	89	6.0	15.8	1
Soybeans, dry	3.5 oz.	100	392	34.3	26.7	3
Tofu, soybean curd, fresh	3.5 oz.	100	72	7.8	2.3	6

N/A—Not available.
N/D—Not determined.

FOOD ITEM	Amount	Grams	Calories	Protein Grams	Carbohydrate Grams	Sodium Mg.
Agé, deep-fried tofu	3.5 oz.	100	346	18.6	4.5	20
Ganmo, tofu patties	3.5 oz.	100	192	15.4	5.1	17
Soybean meal, defatted	3.5 oz.	100	322	49.0	33.6	4
NUTS AND SEEDS						
Almonds, dried, shelled	4 oz.	71	425	13.2	13.8	3
Brazil nuts, shelled	2–3 nuts	10	65	1.4	1.1	N/A
Cashews, shelled	4 oz.	114	639	19.6	33.4	17
Coconut, dry, shredded	4 oz.	31	170	1.1	16.5	N/A
Filberts, shelled	11 nuts	15	95	1.9	2.5	N/A
Peanuts, roasted, salted	8 oz.	144	842	37.4	27.0	602
Peanut butter	1 Tbsp.	14	82	3.5	2.6	85
Pecans, shelled	4 oz.	108	742	9.9	15.8	N/A
Pumpkin seeds	2 oz.	57	315	16.5	8.5	N/A
Sesame seeds	4 oz.	100	616	20.0	N/A	N/A
Sunflower seeds	8 oz.	144	810	15.0	N/A	N/A

N/A—Not available.
N/D—Not determined.

FOOD ITEM	Amount	Grams	Calories	Protein Grams	Carbohydrate Grams	Sodium Mg.
Walnuts, shelled	8 oz.	100	651	14.8	15.8	2
SOME STEWS, COMBINATIONS						
Beef vegetable stew, canned	1 cup	227	179	13.2	16.1	933
Chili con carne, beans, canned	1 cup	227	302	17.0	27.7	1,205
Pizza, baked, frozen	4 oz.	114	279	10.8	40.4	738
Spaghetti, meatballs, sauce	1 cup	227	234	11.1	25.9	1,108
FRUITS						
Apple, fresh	1	150	66	0.2	17.3	2
Apple, dried, cooked	4 oz.	130	101	0.4	26.3	1
Applesauce, canned	4 oz.	119	49	0.3	12.9	2
Apricots, dried	4 oz.	114	296	5.7	75.8	30
Avocados, peeled, pitted	½	108	185	2.4	6.5	4
Banana, 1 medium	6"	150	87	1.1	22.6	1
Banana, dehydrated	1 oz.	28	95	1.2	24.8	1

N/A—Not available.
N/D—Not determined.

FOOD ITEM	Amount	Grams	Calories	Protein Grams	Carbohydrate Grams	Sodium Mg.
Blackberries, raw	4 oz.	122	42	0.8	9.2	1
Blueberries, raw	4 oz.	70	43	0.5	10.7	1
Cantaloupe, 5″ diameter	½	385	58	1.4	14.5	23
Cherries, fresh	8 oz.	130	82	1.5	20.4	3
Citron, candied	1 oz.	28	89	trace	22.4	81
Cranberries, raw	8 oz.	227	100	0.9	23.5	5
Cranberries, dehydrated	1 oz.	28	104	0.8	23.9	5
Currants, raw	8 oz.	114	60	1.9	14.5	3
Dates, pitted	8 oz.	142	389	3.1	103.5	1
Figs, raw	4 oz.	114	91	1.4	23.1	2
Ginger root	1 oz.	28	14	0.4	2.7	2
Ginger, crystallized	1 oz.	28	97	trace	24.6	
Grapefruit, medium	½	285	58	0.7	15.1	1
Grapefruit juice, dehydrated	1 Tbsp.	8	30	0.4	7.2	1
Grapefruit peel, candied	1 oz.	28	90	0.1	22.9	

N/A—Not available.
N/D—Not determined.

FOOD ITEM	Amount	Grams	Calories	Protein Grams	Carbohydrate Grams	Sodium Mg.
Grapes, raw, approx.	8 oz.	160	95	0.9	24.6	4
Guava	4 oz.	114	68	0.9	16.5	5
Lemon, medium	1	106	19	0.8	5.8	1
Lime, medium	1	68	19	0.5	6.5	1
Loganberries, raw	4 oz.	72	45	0.7	10.7	1
Mango, medium	1	303	134	1.4	34.1	14
Nectarine, medium	1	50	30	0.3	7.9	3
Olives, pickled	2 oz.	57	73	0.6	1.5	463
Olives, oiled, Greek-type	2 oz.	57	193	1.2	4.9	1,874
Orange, navel	8 oz.	227	79	2.0	19.6	2
Orange juice, dehydrated	1 Tbsp.	8	30	0.4	7.1	1
Papaya, raw	8 oz.	227	60	0.9	15.2	5
Peach, raw, medium	1	114	35	0.7	10.0	1
Peaches, dried	4 oz.	114	299	3.5	77.9	18
Pear, raw, medium	1	182	100	1.2	25.3	2

N/A—Not available.
N/D—Not determined.

FOOD ITEM	Amount	Grams	Calories	Protein Grams	Carbohydrate Grams	Sodium Mg.
Pears, dried	4 oz.	114	305	3.5	76.7	8
Persimmon, raw, medium	1	125	96	0.9	24.4	6
Pineapple, raw, diced	8 oz.	140	73	0.6	19.2	1
Plum, Damson, raw, medium	1	60	36	0.3	9.7	1
Pomegranate, medium	1	100	63	0.5	16.4	3
Prunes, dried, medium	4	32	82	0.7	21.6	3
Raisins	2 oz.	40	116	1.0	30.9	11
Raspberries, raw	8 oz.	123	90	1.8	19.3	1
Strawberries, raw	4 oz.	75	28	0.5	6.3	
Tangerine, medium	1	114	39	0.78	9.7	2
Watermelon, 4" x 8" wedge	1	925	111	2.1	27.2	4
VEGETABLES						
Alfalfa sprouts	4 oz.	114	20	3.0	3.0	N/A
Bean sprouts, mung	1 cup	90	32	3.4	6.0	4
Bean sprouts, soy	1 cup	107	49	6.6	5.7	N/D

N/A—Not available.
N/D—Not determined.

FOOD ITEM	Amount	Grams	Calories	Protein Grams	Carbohydrate Grams	Sodium Mg.
Beans, green, boiled	½ cup	63	16	1.0	3.3	3
Beets, raw, 2" diameter	1	50	21	0.8	4.9	30
Cabbage, raw, shredded	1 cup	100	24	1.3	5.4	20
Cabbage, Chinese (nappa), raw	1 cup	100	14	1.2	3.0	23
Carrot, raw, medium	1	50	21	0.5	4.8	23
Carrots, dehydrated	1 oz.	28	97	1.9	23.0	76
Celery, raw, stalk	1	40	7	0.4	1.6	50
Chives, raw	4 oz.	114	32	2.0	6.6	N/D
Cucumber, medium	1	207	29	1.2	6.6	12
Dandelion greens, raw	8 oz.	227	102	6.1	20.9	173
Fennel leaves, raw	4 oz.	114	29	2.9	5.4	N/D
Horseradish, prepared	1 oz.	28	11	0.4	2.7	27
Leeks, raw, medium	3	100	52	2.2	11.2	5
Lettuce, iceberg, head	1	454	59	4.1	13.2	41
Lettuce, romaine, leaves	3	28	5	0.4	1.0	3

N/A—Not available.
N/D—Not determined.

FOOD ITEM	Amount	Grams	Calories	Protein Grams	Carbohydrate Grams	Sodium Mg.
Mushrooms, raw	8 oz.	227	61	5.9	9.7	33
Mustard greens, raw	8 oz.	227	49	4.8	8.9	51
Onions, mature, raw	8 oz.	227	79	3.4	17.9	20
Onions, green, small	6	50	22	0.6	5.3	3
Parsley, raw, chopped	1 Tbsp.	4	2	0.1	0.3	2
Peas, green, boiled	½ cup	80	57	4.3	9.6	1
Peppers, sweet green, raw	1	62	14	0.7	3.0	8
Peppers, sweet red, raw	1	60	19	0.8	4.3	N/D
Peppers, green, canned	2 oz.	57	21	0.8	5.2	N/D
Pimientos, canned	1	38	10	0.3	2.2	N/D
Popcorn, plain, popped	1 cup	11	43	1.4	8.4	trace
Potato chips	2 oz.	57	324	3.0	28.5	N/D
Potatoes, white, raw, small	1	100	76	2.1	17.1	3
Potatoes, sweet, baked, med.	1	110	155	2.3	35.7	13
Pumpkin, raw, pulp	4 oz.	114	30	1.1	7.4	1

N/A—Not available.
N/D—Not determined.

FOOD ITEM	Amount	Grams	Calories	Protein Grams	Carbohydrate Grams	Sodium Mg.
Radishes, raw	4	40	7	0.4	1.4	7
Sauerkraut, solid and liquid	4 oz.	114	20	1.1	4.6	N/D
Spinach, raw	8 oz.	227	59	7.3	9.8	161
Squash, boiled	1 cup	210	31	2.1	6.5	2
Squash, acorn, baked	1 cup	205	113	3.9	28.7	2
Tomatoes, raw, medium	1	150	33	1.6	7.0	4
Tomato paste	4 oz.	114	93	3.9	21.2	N/D
Turnip greens, boiled	½ cup	78	18	0.6	3.8	27
Watercress, raw	4 oz.	114	20	2.3	3.1	54
CEREALS, GRAINS, BAKERY FOODS						
Barley, dry	4 oz.	30	175	4.1	39.4	2
Biscuits, canned	4 oz.	114	318	8.3	52.9	990
Bread, Boston brown, slice	1	48	101	2.6	21.9	120
Bread, cracked wheat, slice	1	23	60	2.0	11.9	122
Bread, French, slice	1	20	58	1.8	11.1	116

N/A—Not available.
N/D—Not determined.

FOOD ITEM	Amount	Grams	Calories	Protein Grams	Carbohydrate Grams	Sodium Mg.
Bread, pumpernickel, slice	1	30	74	2.7	15.9	170
Bread, raisin, slice	1	23	60	1.5	12.3	84
Bread, rye, slice	1	23	56	2.1	11.9	128
Bread, white	1	23	62	2.0	11.6	117
Bread, whole wheat, slice	1	23	56	2.4	11.0	121
Cake Mixes:						
Devil's food, dry	4 oz.	114	463	5.5	87.8	521
Gingerbread, dry	4 oz.	114	485	6.2	89.1	528
Yellow, dry (eggs)	4 oz.	114	499	4.6	88.1	464
Cereals, cooking-type:						
Corn grits, dry	¼ cup	40	145	3.5	31.2	trace
Cornmeal, dry	¼ cup	30	166	2.8	22.1	trace
Farina, inst. uncooked	¼ cup	40	145	4.6	30.1	3
Oatmeal, uncooked	¼ cup	20	78	2.8	13.6	trace
Wheat, rolled, uncooked	¼ cup	25	85	2.5	19.1	trace

N/A—Not available.
N/D—Not determined.

FOOD ITEM	Amount	Grams	Calories	Protein Grams	Carbohydrate Grams	Sodium Mg.
Cereals, ready-to-eat:						
Bran flakes, plain	1 oz.	28	86	2.9	22.8	262
Corn flakes, plain	1 oz.	28	109	2.2	24.2	285
Rice flakes, plain	1 oz.	28	110	1.7	24.9	280
Oats, shredded	1 oz.	28	107	5.3	20.4	173
Wheat, shredded, plain	1 oz.	28	100	2.8	22.6	N/D
Cookies:						
Brownies w/nuts, choc.	1 oz.	28	119	1.4	17.2	57
Chocolate chips	1 oz.	28	134	1.5	19.8	114
Fig bars	1 oz.	28	101	1.1	21.4	71
Gingersnaps	1 oz.	28	119	1.6	22.6	162
Macaroons	1 oz.	28	135	1.5	18.7	10
Oatmeal-raisin	1 oz.	28	123	1.8	20.8	46
Shortbread	1 oz.	28	141	2.0	18.4	17
Vanilla wafers	1 oz.	28	131	1.5	21.1	71

N/A—Not available.
N/D—Not determined.

FOOD ITEM	Amount	Grams	Calories	Protein Grams	Carbohydrate Grams	Sodium Mg.
Crackers:						
Graham	1 oz.	28	109	2.3	20.8	190
Soda	1 oz.	28	124	2.6	20.0	312
Whole wheat	1 oz.	28	114	2.4	19.3	155
Zwieback	1 oz.	28	121	2.8	21.8	N/D
Flour, all-purpose	1 cup	122	449	12.2	95.0	N/D
Flour, corn, sifted	1 cup	110	405	8.6	84.5	1
Flour, rye, sifted	1 cup	80	286	7.5	62.3	1
Wheat, all-purpose, sifted	1 cup	110	400	11.5	83.7	2
Macaroni, cooked	1 cup	130	192	6.5	39.1	1
Noodles, cooked	1 cup	160	200	6.6	37.3	3
Noodles, dry, chow-mein	1 oz.	28	139	3.7	16.5	N/D
Spaghetti, dry	1 cup	140	155	4.8	32.2	1
Pancake, 4" diameter	1	45	91	2.7	14.4	203
Piecrust, 9" shell, mix	1	135	675	8.2	59.1	825

N/A—Not available.
N/D—Not determined.

FOOD ITEM	Amount	Grams	Calories	Protein Grams	Carbohydrate Grams	Sodium Mg.
Pretzels	2 oz.	57	222	5.6	43.3	N/D
Rice, brown, cooked	1 cup	168	200	4.2	42.8	321
Rice, white, cooked	1 cup	176	187	3.7	41.0	630
Rice, white, instant, cooked	1 cup	168	183	3.7	40.6	459
SUGARS, FATS, MISCELLANEOUS						
Candies:						
Butterscotch	1 oz.	28	112	trace	26.9	19
Caramel	1 oz.	28	113	1.1	21.7	64
Chocolate, milk	1 oz.	28	135	2.2	13.2	1
Chocolate fudge, nuts	1 oz.	28	121	1.1	19.6	48
Gumdrops	1 oz.	28	98	trace	24.8	10
Marshmallows	1 oz.	28	90	0.6	22.8	11
Peanut brittle	1 oz.	28	119	1.6	23.0	9
Carob powder	1 cup	100	180	4.5	80.7	N/D
Chocolate, baking, unsweetened	2 oz.	57	280	8.0	16.0	6

N/A—Not available.
N/D—Not determined.

FOOD ITEM	Amount	Grams	Calories	Protein Grams	Carbohydrate Grams	Sodium Mg.
Cocoa mix	1 Tbsp.	9	35	0.9	6.6	34
Coconut milk	4 oz.	122	27	0.4	5.7	30
Gelatin, dry, plain	1 Tbsp.	10	33	8.5	0	N/D
Pudding mix, inst. w/milk (chocolate)	½ cup	145	180	4.9	33.1	187
Honey, strained	1 Tbsp.	21	64	trace	17.3	1
Jellies, all	1 Tbsp.	20	55	trace	14.3	3
Sugar, brown, packed	1 cup	220	821	0	212.1	66
Sugar, granulated	1 cup	200	770	0	199.0	2
Sugar, powdered	1 Tbsp.	20	53	0	8.0	trace
Sauce, soy	1 Tbsp.	14	9	0.8	1.2	1,025
Sauce, Tabasco	¼ tsp.	1	0	0.9	1.1	5
Salt	1 tsp.	4	0	0	0	1,550
Fats:						
Butter, salted	1 Tbsp.	14	100	0.1	trace	138
Butter, unsalted	1 Tbsp.	14	100	0.1	trace	1

N/A—Not available.
N/D—Not determined.

FOOD ITEM	Amount	Grams	Calories	Protein Grams	Carbohydrate Grams	Sodium Mg.
Butter, salted	8 oz.	227	1,625	1.4	0.9	2,240
Butter, unsalted	8 oz.	227	1,625	1.4	0.9	22
Margarine, salted	1 Tbsp.	14	101	0.1	trace	138
Margarine, unsalted	1 Tbsp.	14	101	0.1	trace	1
Margarine, salted	8 oz.	227	1,634	1.4	0.9	2,240
Margarine, unsalted	8 oz.	227	1,634	1.4	0.9	22
Salad oils	1 Tbsp.	14	124	0	0	0
Lard	8 oz.	205	1,850	0	0	0
Mayonnaise	1 Tbsp.	15	108	0.2	0.3	90

N/A—Not available.
N/D—Not determined.

ADDITIVES

THE LABEL WATCH: WHAT IS IN OUR FOOD?

Additives in food are widespread, but information about their safety is difficult to obtain. Here are some of the chemicals—those to avoid, those that *may be* safe, and those that *are* safe for human consumption. Some people are more allergic to the effects of the various additives than others.

Sugar (sucrose, glucose, fructose) and salt (sodium) are widely used and popular seasonings, but may cause nutritional imbalances in very large quantities. The hidden amounts of sugar and salt in processed foods are often hard to establish.

The lists that follow are not complete, but show the chemicals most widely used in processed foods.

CHEMICALS TO AVOID

ARTIFICIAL COLORINGS: Blue No. 1; Blue No. 2; Citrus Red No. 2; Green No. 3; Orange B; Red No. 3; Red No. 40; Yellow No. 5.

BROMINATED VEGETABLE OIL (BVO): An emulsifier and antioxidant.

SODIUM NITRITE, SODIUM NITRATE: Preservatives, coloring, flavoring. Used in bacon, ham, smoked fish, corned beef, other processed meats.

CHEMICALS THAT MAY BE SAFE

BUTYLATED HYDROXYANISOLE (BHA): An antioxidant. Retards rancidity in fats.

HEPTYL PARABEN: A preservative. Used as a preservative in some beers.

HYDROGENATED VEGETABLE OIL: Vegetable oil, usually liquid, can be made semisolid by treatment with hydrogen. Converts much of polyunsaturated oil to saturated fat, about which there is question as to value or danger in the daily diet. Additive needs better testing.

Monosodium glutamate (MSG): A flavor enhancer to which many people are allergic. Used primarily in Oriental foods, seasonings.

Phosphoric acid, phosphates: Phosphoric acid flavors cola beverages. Phosphate salts are used for many purposes. Calcium and iron phosphates are mineral supplements. Sodium aluminum phosphate is a leavening agent. Calcium and ammonium phosphates serve as food for yeast. Sodium acid pyrophosphate prevents discoloration in potatoes and sugar syrups. Phosphates are not toxic, but widespread use may cause dietary imbalances.

Propyl gallate: An antioxidant. Has not been adequately tested. Often used with BHA and BHT to help retard rancidity. Should be avoided.

Sulfur dioxide, sodium bisulfite: Preservative, bleach. Prevents discoloration in dried fruits. Destroys Vitamin B-1, but is otherwise safe.

CHEMICALS CONSIDERED SAFE

Alginate, propylene glycol alginate: Foam stabilizers, thickening agents. Alginate is a derivative of seaweed (kelp). Propylene glycol alginate is a chemically modified alginate.

Alpha tocopherol (*Vitamin E*): Antioxidant, nutrient.

Ascorbic acid (*Vitamin C*): Antioxidant, nutrient.

Beta carotene: Coloring and nutrient which the body converts to Vitamin A.

Calcium (or sodium) propionate: Preservative, prevents mold in breads.

Calcium (or sodium) stearoyl lactylate: Dough conditioner in breads.

CARRAGEENAN: Thickening and stabilizing agent. Obtained from "Irish moss" seaweed, it stabilizes oil-water mixtures.

CASEIN, SODIUM CASEINATE: Thickening and whitening agent. Casein, the principal protein in milk, is nutritious, contains amounts of all essential amino acids.

CITRIC ACID, SODIUM CITRATE: Acid, flavoring. Citric acid is widely used, cheap and safe. Found in citrus fruits. Sodium citrate, also safe, controls the acidity of gelatin desserts, jams, other foods.

EDTA: Chelating agent. EDTA traps metallic impurities in manufactured foods which could promote rancidity and breakdown of artificial colors. (Ethylenediamine tetracetic acid.)

FERROUS GLUCONATE: Coloring, nutrient. Used to blacken olives and as a source of iron in pills.

FUMARIC ACID: Tartness agent. An ideal source of tartness and acidity in dry food products.

GELATIN: Thickening and gelling agent. A protein obtained from animal bones, hoofs, and other parts. Has nutritional value but lacks some essential amino acids.

GLYCERIN (GLYCEROL): Glycerin forms the backbone of fat and oil molecules and is quite safe. The body uses it as a source of energy or as a basic material in making more complex molecules.

GUMS, GUAR, LOCUST BEAN, ARABIC, FURCELLERAN, GHATTI, KARAYA, TRAGACANTH: Thickening agents, stabilizers. Gums derived from natural vegetable sources are poorly tested, but are probably safe. Used to thicken foods, form a gel in puddings, keep oil and water mixed in salad dressings.

HYDROLYZED VEGETABLE PROTEIN (HVP): Flavor enhancer. HVP consists of vegetable (usually soybean) protein that has been chemically broken down to the amino acids of which it is composed. HVP is used to bring out natural flavors of foods and to substitute for real food.

LACTIC ACID: Acidity regulator. This safe acid occurs in almost all living organisms. It inhibits spoilage in olives, balances acidity in cheese making, adds tartness to frozen desserts, carbonated drinks, other foods.

LACTOSE: A sweetener. A carbohydrate found only in milk. Nature's way to deliver calories to infant mammals. One-sixth as sweet as granulated sugar, it is added to foods as a slightly sweet source of carbohydrate. Milk turns sour when bacteria convert lactose to lactic acid.

LECITHIN: Emulsifier and antioxidant. A common constituent of animal and plant tissues; a source of the nutrient choline. Keeps oil and water together, retards acidity. Major sources are egg yolk, soybeans.

MANNITOL: Sweetener. Not as sweet as sugar, and contains only half as many calories. Used to "dust" chewing gum, prevent foods from becoming sticky.

MONO- AND DI-GLYCERIDES: Emulsifiers. Make bread softer and prevent staleness; prevent oil in peanut butter from separating.

POLYSORBATE 60: Emulsifier. Same uses as mono- and di-glycerides. Synthetic, but appears to be safe.

SODIUM BENZOATE: Preservative. Long used to prevent growth of bacteria in acidic foods.

SODIUM CARBOXYMETHYLCELLULOSE: Thickening agent. Made by treating cellulose with a derivative of acetic acid (vinegar).

SORBIC ACID, POTASSIUM SORBATE: Prevents growth of mold and bacteria. Sorbic acid usually occurs in berries of the mountain ash. Sorbate may be a safe replacement for sodium nitrite in bacon.

SORBITAN MONOSTEARATE: Emulsifier. Keeps oil and water from separating.

SORBITOL: Sweetener, thickening agent. Sorbitol occurs naturally in fruits and berries and is a relative of the sugars. Large amounts (2 oz.) have a laxative effect, but it is safe. Diabetics use sorbitol because it is absorbed slowly and does not cause blood sugar to increase rapidly.

STARCH, MODIFIED STARCH: Thickening agent. Major component of flour, potatoes, corn. Does not dissolve in cold water, so chemists modify starch with various chemicals. Makes sauces appear thicker and richer than they really are.

VANILLIN, ETHYL VANILLIN: Substitute for vanilla. Vanilla is a bean, but vanillin is cheaper to produce synthetically. Vanillin is safe. Ethyl vanillin needs to be better tested.

PACKAGING AND STORAGE

Frozen mammoths found in melting glaciers are the best example of long-term food storage. Even with freezing, fats become rancid over a period of time. After a year in the freezer, the fat in meat will become rancid and will have developed a musky flavor.

Freeze-dried foods last longer, but also become rancid after a year of storage. These foods are edible, but require more seasoning to make them palatable, to mask the musky, rancid flavor that inevitably occurs.

The keeping qualities of most foods are generally overrated, particularly those of grains. The oils in grains become rancid after several months' storage, unless the grains or beans are kept refrigerated. Vacuum-packed and unopened packaged foods have a longer shelf-life, as long as the package remains sealed and the air does not reach it. Carefully consider the keeping of any freeze-dried or dehydrated packaged food longer than a year, even in the freezer. Foods do deteriorate, and with deterioration, form unpleasant acids that may harm the human body. The fresher the food when eaten, the better the body receives it.

For outings away from refrigeration, we are faced with the necessity of using dried fruits, vegetables, and meats. Canned and bottled foods properly sealed keep longer than frozen and dried foods, but even they should not be kept over a year without careful checking to be sure spoilage has not occurred.

Dried foods should be stored in tins or sealed plastic bags on cool, dark shelves away from heat and light. Package them in individual daily or weekly servings, and place label inside the outer bag showing the name of the item, its weight, and use.

Vegetables and meats to be used in main-dish soups or stews should be packaged in the amounts required for specific dishes.

Foods stored in plastic will absorb the flavor of the plastic after a few months. If longer storage is necessary, foil and waxed paper, or tins, make better wrappings for such foods. Frozen meats and other items should be wrapped in waxed paper or foil, then placed in plastic bags, if desired. The date of storage should be put on the label to be sure the items is not kept too long. Most frozen foods may be kept for six months to a year.

PACKAGING FOR THE TRAIL

Dry foods may be packed in plastic bags and tied with rubber bands. It is best to double-bag the items, slipping a label describing the food and its purpose between the bags, for easy identification. Remove as much air from the food bag as possible before sealing it.

Dried milk should be packaged in one-quart amounts for ease of use. Package milk to be used with puddings or soups with the packages of food in which the milk will be used. Place all of the packages in a larger bag, properly identified and tied, with as little air as possible.

STAPLES

Dry staples—such as coffee, cocoa, sugar, powdered milk, flour for breads, and others—should be packaged in plastic jars, properly labeled, or in double plastic bags with the label inside the outer bag, both fastened with rubber bands.

Herbs and other dry seasonings may be stored in small plastic bottles or 35-mm film cans, properly labeled and placed in a plastic bag of suitable size.

Liquid, moist, and oily items such as salad oil, vinegar, mayonnaise, peanut butter, and honey, should be packed in screw-top plastic jars, labeled, and placed in a plastic bag for additional safety.

Liquid margarine is available and convenient. Butter may be clarified (melted and the white milk solid removed) and poured into a screw-top bottle or jar. Neither will spoil but, if left in the sun, they become rancid more quickly, as do all fats. Mayonnaise may be kept in jars for a week or more and must also be kept in a cool place, in the pack or in camp.

Matches should be placed in waterproof containers, or in plastic bags. Cleaning pads, bar soap, and brush should be packed in a plastic bag. Toilet paper and other items should be stored in plastic bags.

List all items needed, the amounts per day, then total for the number of days of the trip, to be sure all items have been purchased. Check menus and recipes for all meals to be sure every item is accounted for and packaged.

SAFETY AND PERISHABLES

Frozen fresh meats and vegetables may be taken along, well wrapped and insulated against heat, for the first night in camp. Fresh milk may be frozen, wrapped well, and taken along for the first night. In cold weather, or where snowbanks and cold streams are close by, fresh meats may be kept until the second night. Vegetables will keep fresh longer if they are crisped in cold water before serving. Cooked meats, frozen and carefully packaged, are easy to take along for first and second nights, if they are kept cold or frozen until needed.

To freeze eggs: Stir slightly without adding air, add 1 teaspoon salt, pour into plastic container and freeze. To use, thaw, and beat.

Cooked eggs should be eaten the day of preparation, as should any spreads or salads mixed with mayonnaise, which also contains egg. Raw eggs, packed in a carton, will keep as long as a week if the shells remain uncracked. On hot days, wrap the carton in a wet cloth, then in plastic bag for keeping in the backpack.

Cheese, curds, butter, and yoghurt were developed thousands of years ago as methods for preserving milk, so that the resulting products would be safe to eat, and keep without refrigeration.

Modern soft cheeses and sour cream will mold within a week or ten days even in the refrigerator. Kept from the heat of the sun, these products will keep their consistency and remain edible for at least three or four days on the trail. All fats become rancid in time, and heat speeds the process. Chilled foods retain their firmness, are easier to handle, and are more palatable to modern eyes and tastes.

The bean curd, tofu, is not a fermented product but must be kept in a plastic container with fresh water to cover the curd. It will keep for three or four days on the trail or in camp.

To protect perishable and semiperishable foods from heat, take the items chilled from the refrigerator and tie into plastic bags, then wrap in sweaters, wool socks, or down boots, and place in the center of the backpack. Packages of frozen meats for the first night's dinner, cartons of frozen milk, or plastic bottles of frozen fruit juices or water, may be packaged with soft cheeses, salad and sandwich mixtures, or other milk products and fats to keep them chilled during the day. The milk will remain sweet into the second day. If it sours, it may be used for cooking.

In camp, either day or night, eggs, meats, and milk products should be placed in a wet cloth or burlap sack and hung from a tree limb. This method permits the air to circulate, and the evaporation keeps the foods cool. If no trees are available, place the bag on rocks at the edge of a stream or lake, in the shade. If no shade is available during the day, place the packages in sleeping bags. The foods will not spoil or become rancid as quickly when protected from the sun.

There are small insulated bags available for those who prefer them. The larger Styrofoam coolers are useful for boat trips, car camping or base camps but are not used for backpacking.

The symbol ✿ beside a recipe in this book indicates that it uses perishable ingredients that require the protective measures described.

MILK-MATE: A tablespoon of coffee creamer mixed with dry milk improves the flavor.

Richard Allen
Port Washington, New York

EQUIPMENT

A reasonable minimum of equipment for two backpackers—for convenience, not bare necessity—is listed below.

> 1 stove
> 1 one-quart pot, with lid, to provide 1 pint liquid per person
> 1 one-pint pot, with lid, for extra hot water
> 1 metal pot lifter, or small pliers
> 1 small wooden spoon, long enough to reach bottom of largest pot
> 1 small spatula
> 1 griddle or frying pan (optional)
> 1 folding plastic bag or bucket for water
> 3 or 4 feet heavy-grade aluminum foil
> 1 padded glove for handling hot pots
> 1 or 2 steel wool or copper scrubbing pads
> 1 metal cup, spoon, pocket knife for each person
> 1 plastic bowl for each person (a convenience)
> Plastic bags for pots and food

Sets of aluminum pots usually come in threes, nesting, with flat lids, or with rounded lids with folding handles. Frying-pan lids provide extra utensils with minimum weight.

THROWAWAY PLATE: Take a Frisbee along on a trip. Makes a fair dinner plate, and after washing up, toss it to someone.

Ed Jensen
Cornelius, Oregon

WALKING WITH A WOK

An interesting and useful alternative to one pot and a frying pan is the *wok,* an Oriental cooking utensil that resembles a round-bottomed frying pan. It is used for stir-frying and steaming vegetables and other foods. Supported by a metal ring, or one made of aluminum foil, a wok can easily be used on park fireplaces. A 5-pint steel wok weighs a bit over 1 pound, without lid, and will not fit on *small* camp stoves. Aluminum foil may be used as a lid.

ALUMINUM FOIL

Heavy-grade foil may be shaped into bowls, wrapped around a forked stick, to provide an instant lightweight frying pan. Or, if time and interest permit, a piece of foil may be set at an angle behind a pan of bread beside a fire or stove, to provide a reflector oven. If the sun is hot, make a wide, shallow bowl of foil, set the food in the middle, and try solar cooking. This method works best on a hot rock or desert sand.

BACKPACKING WITHOUT A STOVE

It also is possible to travel for days with *no stove*—with fruit, water, and foods prepared at home. Water is the most important item, with fruit juice and concentrated foods next in importance, especially in hot weather.

THE BACKPACK STOVE

The choice of stoves is an individual matter. Needs and personal preferences should be considered before investing in expensive equipment. *Backpacker Magazine* has tested many stoves and has provided some guidelines for selecting a stove.

1. PRICE. Stoves may be simple or complex. Models with no moving parts or valves sell for as little as $2 or $3. Butane and propane stoves may sell between $10 and $30. White-gas models cost more—between $18 and $60.
2. WEIGHT. Stoves tested ranged between 1½ ounces and 3 pounds 5 ounces. The larger stoves are best used by parties of at

least four people. Lighter models, which cook more slowly, are suited to solitary backpackers, who rarely need to boil more than a few cups of water at a time.

Fuel weight is a consideration, too. On a week-long trip for four, 84 quarts of water may be boiled. Weight versus power must be considered. The 3-pound 5-ounce Optimus 111B boils water three times faster than the 10-ounce Prolite Pocket stove, but it is five times heavier.

3. EASE OF PACKING. Compactness and absence of sharp edges are important. As with weight, there is a relationship between size and efficiency. The larger the stove, the greater the heat. Stoves that fit into cooking pots or protective cases are convenient to pack.

4. DURABILITY. Exposed parts break easily. Multiple parts or fittings may loosen, fall off and get lost. The stove should be packed carefully in a pot, case, or sack. Treat with care.

5. SAFETY. Handle stoves carefully. Some are safer than others, and construction must be considered.

Tank placement is important. Fuel tanks must not be too close to burners.

Fuel volatility must be considered. Propane, butane, and white gas are incendiary explosives and must be treated with respect. Kerosene and a few solids are less volatile. Denatured alcohol ignites but with a cooler, more wavering flame than other liquid fuels. Stoves are *dangerous* and must be treated with care and respect.

Starting a fire can be dangerous if the stove flares. The hazard with liquid fuels is minimal unless you are careless or prime the stove with too much fuel. With some butane stoves, flare can be unpredictable and thus more dangerous than with other models.

Refueling a cold stove must be done carefully. Tanks should be accessible. Detaching cartridges on butane and propane tanks is also dangerous. The Bleuet-type cartridge appears to be the safest because it is not disconnected every time the stove is used.

Fuel connections may be poorly designed, milled, welded, and fitted. Check before buying.

6. STABILITY. A safety function, governed by five design factors: height of stove, width of base, width of pot supports, weight, and location of weight concentration. Short, wide stoves with sturdy pot supports are safest, most stable when topped by a full pot.

7. RELIABILITY. A multiplicity of screw-in parts to come loose or bind, is a sign of unreliability. Quality of metals and welding is another thing to look for. Stainless steel and brass, heavier-than-

aluminum alloys, plastic, and rubber, are also more reliable. Alloy fittings may loosen or freeze after repeated heating and cooling. Often close scrutiny will be enough to detect sloppy welding.

8. COLD-WEATHER PERFORMANCE. Cold weather makes most stoves harder to start, slower to burn. When temperatures drop below freezing at sea level, butane will not vaporize. Even above freezing, the cartridges will be so cool that they push out gas more slowly. The liquid-feed models are not susceptible to this problem until about 10°F.; then they flare more than usual during start-up. Propane vaporizes and burns far below 0°F. White gas and kerosene perform equally well. With liquid fuel, priming may be more tedious on models without pumps. If the tank is far below the burner, and has no pump, it may lose pressure and go out during use. Select a stove for the worst possible conditions. A windscreen will aid performance no matter what the weather conditions or altitude.

Wind and altitude will always affect stove performance. At high elevations, air density and the amount of oxygen available for combustion decrease. A stove must take in enough oxygen to burn with the fuel vapors it releases. If not, it runs too rich (as a car does), wastes fuel, and burns with a cooler, yellow-tipped flame.

9. CLEANING. Kerosene stoves accumulate soot; white-gas models do to a lesser extent, mostly in and above the priming cup. Butane and propane units are immaculate. Prevent plugging of white-gas jets. Some white-gas models come with a probe needle which should be poked into the jet every day or so. Others have built-in needles controlled by the burner knob.

10. NOISE. All white-gas and kerosene stoves roar—some louder than others. Propane and butane stoves whisper. Sterno and Heat Tabs are silent.

11. QUALITY OF INSTRUCTIONS. A good set of instructions should cover starting, running use, troubleshooting, and spare-parts availability.

12. ENVIRONMENTAL CONCERNS. Stoves should be instruments of conservation. Fires are prohibited in many national and state parks, but canister litter has become prevalent. The careful backpacker carries out his canisters with other garbage.

13. KINDS OF FUEL AND AVAILABILITY.

White gas is a special, additive-free version of automobile gasoline; it is often difficult to find.

Coleman fuel, carried in hardware stores, sporting-goods stores, and many backpacking shops, is a cleaner fuel. It contains rust inhibitors and additives which make for easier lighting and faster burning. Neither is commonly found abroad.

Cold weather affects gas less; the most efficient heating stoves (MSR, Optimus 111B, Phoebus 625) use it. Must be used with great care to prevent flaring.

Kerosene is less volatile and burns hotter than white gas. However, it is smelly, smoky, and hard to start. It is easy to find in odd corners of the world, and is relatively cheap. Optimus 00 and 45, and the MSR multifuel model run on kerosene. Hardware stores usually carry kerosene.

Butane and *propane* come in pressurized steel canisters. Under pressure, both are liquid. As they leave the canisters, they vaporize and expand 270 times in volume.

Butane and propane stoves operate simply: push or screw canisters into the stove. (Hold screw-top upright while screwing into stove.) Both fuels start quickly, at the touch of a match and a turn of the stove's control knob. Both burn more cleanly than gas. Canisters *are not safer than white gas.* If a poor connection is made, leakage and explosion can occur. *All stoves demand safe handling.*

In cold weather, propane will vaporize down to minus 44°F. Butane will not vaporize below 32°F. Propane is a better cold-weather fuel, and steel canisters are stronger and heavier. Canisters for the Coleman 5418 and Kangaroo Trail Boss weigh 2 pounds when full. But for light cooking under benign conditions, butane is superior. Standard butane canisters, such as those used for the Bleuet, weigh 9½ ounces and are found in most backpacking shops. Optimus and EFI cartridges are found less often, and Prolite is generally hard to find. Propane cartridges are found in most general sporting-goods stores.

Denatured alcohol is burned by two stoves: Optimus 45A and a small model marketed by REI. Alcohol burns coolly compared to gas or kerosene. For the same weight, it produces only half as much heat. In addition, it costs more. The advantage of alcohol is its low volatility, a strong safety feature. Unlike most fuels, alcohol is not a petroleum product. It may be found in most hardware stores.

Solid fuels such as Sterno, charcoal, and heat tabs, are safer than other fuels, but have lower heating power. *Sterno,* a gelatinous substance used in chafing dishes, is found in hardware stores. A stove frame for the Sterno can is available for around $2.00. A more expensive solid-fuel stove, the *Zip Stove* burns charcoal, twigs, wood chips, pine cones, or yak dung. An AC battery runs the fan that starts the flame and keeps it going, if necessary. Heat tabs are available in several brands: *Heat Tabs, Hexzmine, Esbit Fuel Tabs,* and *Speaker Heat Tabs* (the latter available only from Speaker Corporation, Milwaukee, Wisconsin). These may be used for priming gas stoves, as well. Solid-fuel stoves are useful for roadheads or for short trips.

HOW TO USE YOUR STOVE SAFELY

Stoves are dangerous, and knowledge of the dangers is essential. If it is necessary to cook inside a tent, extra care must be taken. *Flare* while starting is only one hazard. Even more dangerous are the risks of *asphyxiation* and *carbon monoxide poisoning.* More winter camping deaths occur from these causes than from any other. If ventilation is inadequate, a burning stove will use up all the oxygen in a tent very quickly. Using a stove in a confined space can be as lethal as being in a closed garage with a car motor running. Stoves give off deadly carbon monoxide gas. Use common sense and the safety precautions listed.

• Try the stove at home. Learn to operate it, test it carefully.
• Cook outside the tent. If you *must* cook inside, open the tent flap slightly, even if the vent is open. Fresh air is vital! (True of lanterns and hand warmers as well).
• Place the stove in a safe place, on a level surface, away from burnable materials.
• Don't overfill fuel tank. If too full, it can build up pressure while cooking.
• Don't overprime, as it can cause a large flare-up. Use an eye-dropper. A bottle of alcohol is a safe primer, as are heat tabs.
• Replace fuel cap before priming.
• Close fuel-regulating valve while priming.
• Don't spill fuel. If you do, clean it up carefully *at once.*
• Use the correct fuel for the stove.
• Don't use oversize pots on a stove.
• Avoid overheating the fuel tank. Check it from time to time. It should be cool. If it is hot, turn off stove at once.
• With flexible fuel tubes, keep tank as far away from stove as possible.
• Always be sure stove is sufficiently ventilated so that fresh air can circulate around the bottom.

- In a wind, be sure flame is not blowing toward fuel tank.
- Turn off stove if it is not working properly. Remove pot, check stove carefully, and do not use it if trouble persists.
- Refuel away from open flames.
- Turn off stove before checking fuel level or cartridge connections.
- Do not fuel a hot stove. *Let it cool* before refueling.
- Replace gas canisters carefully. If a cartridge is difficult to screw in, don't force it. Be sure the connection is secure.
- If you hear a faint hiss when you attach a new cartridge for a propane or butane stove, there may be a leak. If gas continues to leak, replace cartridge.
- To check for a leak, feel the tank. Even a pinprick will cause the tank to feel frosty. *Do not shake the canister.*
- Replace caps on fuel bottles carefully and firmly after refueling. Place bottles several feet away from the stove before lighting.
- Be sure discarded canisters are empty before putting in trash. And, pack the cartridge out with your trash.
- Clean the stove according to manufacturer's directions. Build-up of soot and grease will interfere with stove's performance.
- Treat stove with care; *it is delicate.* If it is dropped, check it carefully before using.
- *Keep cool.* Don't panic if there is an accident. A small flare-up can get out of hand if you panic and push the stove away or throw it—*especially in a tent.*

More information about stoves and their use may be found in *Backpacker Magazine,* Nos. 15, 16, and 32.

MEASUREMENTS AND WEIGHTS

COMMON EQUIVALENTS

1 teaspoon	= ⅙ fluid ounce	
3 teaspoons	= 1 tablespoon	
4 tablespoons	= ¼ cup	
16 tablespoons	= 1 cup	
2 cups	= 1 pint	= 16 fluid ounces
4 cups	= 1 quart	= 32 fluid ounces
4 quarts	= 1 gallon	
8 quarts	= 1 peck	

COMMON EQUIVALENTS

16 ounces	= 1 pound
1 quart, dry weight	= 22 ounces
1 gallon water	= 8.33 pounds

APPROXIMATE MEASUREMENTS OF COMMONLY USED FOODS

Almonds, shelled, 1 pound	= 3 cups
Apples, fresh, 1 pound	= 2 or 3 apples
Apples, dried, 1 pound	= 5 cups
Apricots, 1 pound	= 3 to $3\frac{1}{2}$ cups
Bacon, 1 pound	= 16 thin slices
Bananas, 1 pound	= 3 bananas, medium
Beets, 1 pound	= 2 or 3 beets
Brazil nuts, shelled, 1 pound	= 3 cups
Bread, 1-pound loaf	= 16 slices
Butter, 1 pound	= 2 cups
Butter, 1 stick	= $\frac{1}{4}$ pound or $\frac{1}{2}$ cup or 8 tablespoons
Carrots, 1 pound	= 3 to 5 carrots
Chocolate, 1 pound	= 16 squares
1 square	= 1 ounce
Coffee (ground), 1 pound	= 5 cups
Cranberries, 1 pound	= 4 cups
Cream, thick	= doubles in whipping
Dates, dried, 1 pound	= 3 to $3\frac{1}{2}$ cups
Dates, fresh, 1 pound	= 2 cups
Eggs, fresh	
4 to 6 whole eggs	= 1 cup
8 to 10 egg whites	= 1 cup
12 to 14 egg yolks	= 1 cup
Eggs, dried	

  Whole egg: $2\frac{1}{2}$ tablespoons plus $2\frac{1}{2}$ tablespoons water = 1 egg
  Egg white: 2 teaspoons plus 2 tablespoons water = 1 egg white
  Egg yolk: 2 tablespoons plus 2 teaspoons water = 1 egg yolk

Figs, dried, 1 pound	= 3 to $3\frac{1}{2}$ cups
Figs, fresh, 1 pound	= 2 cups
Fruits and peels, candied	
1 pound	= 2 cups
Flour (white), 1 pound	= 4 cups
Lemons, juice of 1 medium	= 4 tablespoons
Margarine, 1 pound	= 2 cups
Onions, 1 pound	= 4 to 12 onions
Peaches, fresh, 1 pound	= 3 to 5 peaches
Peaches, dried, 1 pound	= 3 to $3\frac{1}{2}$ cups
Potatoes, white, 1 pound	= 2 to 4 potatoes
Potatoes, sweet; yams, 1 pound	= 2 to 3 potatoes

Raisins, 1 pound	= 3 cups
Shortening, 1 pound	= 2 cups
Spinach, 1 pound	= 3 to 4 servings
String beans, 1 pound	= 4 servings
Sugar, granulated, 1 pound	= 2 cups
Sugar, brown, packed,	
¾ pound	= 2 cups
Tomatoes, 1 pound	= 2 to 5 tomatoes
Walnuts, shelled, 1 pound	= 2 cups

FREEZE-DRIED FOODS, APPROXIMATE SERVINGS PER PERSON

Meats	1–1.5 ounces
Green beans	0.25 ounces
Cabbage	0.4–0.5 ounces
Carrots	0.4–0.5 ounces
Corn or peas	0.5–0.6 ounces
Apples, other fruits	1 ounce
Strawberries	0.5–0.6 ounces

METRIC CONVERSION—VOLUME

5 milliliters	= 1 teaspoon, approximately
15 milliliters	= 1 tablespoon, approximately
250 milliliters	= 1 cup, approximately
1 liter	= 2.11 pints (4 cups, approximately)
1 liter	= 1.06 quarts
1 liter	= 0.26 gallons
3.78 liters	= 1 gallon
29.57 milliliters	= 1 fluid ounce

To convert:

Teaspoons	× 5	= milliliters
Tablespoons	× 15	= milliliters
Fluid ounces	× 29.57	= milliliters
Cups	× 0.24	= liters
Pints	× 0.47	= liters
Quarts	× 0.95	= liters
Gallons	× 3.78	= liters
Milliliters	× 0.2	= teaspoons
Milliliters	× 0.6	= tablespoons
Milliliters	× 0.03	= fluid ounces
Milliliters	× 0.004	= cups
Liters	× 0.42	= cups
Liters	× 2.11	= pints
Liters	× 1.06	= quarts
Liters	× 0.26	= gallons

METRIC CONVERSION—WEIGHT

1,000 milligrams	= 1 gram
28.35 grams	= 1 ounce
1 kilogram	= 2.2 pounds
250 grams	= 9 ounces
500 grams	= 1.1 pounds

To convert:

Ounces	× 28.35	= grams
Pounds	× 0.45	= kilograms
Grams	× 0.035	= ounces
Kilograms	× 2.20	= pounds

METRIC CONVERSION—TEMPERATURES

Boiling point of water = 212° Fahrenheit = 100° Celsius
Freezing point of water = 32° Fahrenheit = 0° Celsius

To convert:

Degrees Fahrenheit	= (9/5 × degrees Celsius) + 32
Degrees Celsius	= 5/9 × (degrees Fahrenheit − 32)

ALTITUDE ADJUSTMENTS—BOILING

At 5,000 feet, the temperature of boiling water is 9.5°F. lower than it is at sea level. Beverages must be made with furiously boiling water and allowed to steep longer than at sea level, and cooking times must be increased for soups, stews, cereals, meats, and vegetables. Add extra water to make up for evaporation.

Elevation	Boiling Point of Water (°F.)
0 ft. (sea level)	212.0°
500	211.0°
1,000	210.0°
1,500	209.1°
2,000	208.2°
2,500	207.1°
3,000	206.2°
3,500	205.3°
4,000	204.4°
4,500	203.4°
5,000	202.6°
5,500	201.7°
6,000	200.7°

Elevation	*Boiling Point of Water (°F.)*
6,500	199.8°
7,000	198.7°
7,500	198.0°
8,000	196.9°
10,000	194.0°
12,500	189.8°
14,000	187.3°

ALTITUDE ADJUSTMENTS—BAKING

Ingredients	*2,000 to 3,500 ft.*	*3,500 to 5,500 ft.*	*5,000 to 6,500 ft.*	*6,500 to 8,000 ft.*
Decrease each teaspoon baking powder, baking soda, cream of tartar	¼– ⅓ tsp.	⅓– ½ tsp.	½– ⅔ tsp.	⅔– 1 tsp.
Decrease each cup sugar	1– 1½ tbsp.	1½– 2½ tbsp.	2½– 3 tbsp.	3– 3½ tbsp.
Increase each cup liquid	0– 2 tbsp.	2– 3 tbsp.	3– 4 tbsp.	4– 6 tbsp.
Increase cake flour	—	1 tbsp.	2 tbsp.	3 tbsp.
Increase baking temp.	—	15°F.– 25°F.	15°F.– 25°F.	25°F.

1. Very rich cake batters will be lighter if fat is decreased 1–2 tablespoons.
2. Follow any high-altitude instruction on recipes of cake mixes.
3. Do not overbeat batter or eggs. An extra egg will stabilize batter.
4. Grease pans well—cakes are more likely to stick at high altitudes.
5. Dry cakes may be prevented by adding more liquid to batters or dough.
6. Do not raise heat to try to cook faster. Lower heat to prevent burning.

OVEN TEMPERATURE TESTS

If no thermometer is available, an approximate test of an oven's heat may be made in this way:

When the oven is heated, lay a piece of white paper on the lower shelf. Various kinds of paper brown differently:

1. If the paper becomes light brown in 5 minutes, it is a *slow* oven (250°F.–350°F.)
2. If the paper becomes medium brown in 5 minutes, it is a *moderate* oven (350°F.–400°F.)
3. If the paper becomes dark brown in 5 minutes, it is a *hot* oven (400°F.–500°F.)

HIGH-ALTITUDE OVEN TEMPERATURES

Oven	*Degrees Fahrenheit*	*Degrees Centigrade*
Slow	300°F.–325°F.	149°C.–163°C.
Moderate	340°F.–375°F.	177°C.–191°C.
Hot	400°F.–425°F.	204°C.–218°C.

If you plan to do a great deal of high-altitude baking, invest in a book devoted to the subject. There are several on the market. See Bibliography (p. 305).

HELPFUL TIPS FOR THE TRAIL

INSECT BITES

WILD ONIONS: Rub juice of wild onion leaves on skin to discourage mosquitoes and other insects from biting.

MEAT TENDERIZER: If insects ignore onion juice and bite, stop the itching by applying powdered meat tenderizer to damp skin. Carry it in 35mm. film cans for handy use.

BAKING SODA: Rub baking soda on mosquito bites or bee stings to reduce itching and swelling. Carry the soda in a 35mm. film can.

POISON OAK AND POISON IVY

NAPHTHA SOAP: After contact with poison oak and poison ivy, wash well *immediately* with naphtha soap. It is more effective in washing off irritating oils than other soaps.

TOOTH POWDER AND DEODORANT

BAKING SODA: Use soda alone or mixed with salt as a tooth powder. Wash with it, and use it as a deodorant.

Beverages

BARLEY "COFFEE"

AT HOME:
Buy whole barley at natural-food stores.

Spread 2 or 3 layers on a baking sheet and roast 30 to 45 minutes in a 350°F. oven, or until the seeds are a deep brown. Stir several times to ensure even browning.

Grind barley in a blender or coffee grinder as needed. Store in a tin. Package in plastic bag the amount needed for an outing.

IN CAMP:
Bring water to a boil; add 1 rounded tablespoon of ground barley per cup of water. Lower heat, boil 3 minutes, and remove from heat. Let grounds settle. Drink black, or with cream and sugar.

REAL COFFEE

AT HOME:
Package regular or drip coffee in a small tin, for the number of persons and days on the outing. Coffee absorbs flavor of plastic; *do not use plastic bags*.

IN CAMP:
Put 1 tablespoon of coffee grounds per cup into a pot of cold water. Bring water to boil, and boil for 1 minute. Remove pot from stove and flick a few drops of cold water into the top of the brew to settle grounds. Let set, covered, for 3 minutes. Carefully pour into cups without stirring up grounds from bottom of the pot.

Seymour C. Treadwell
Bara, Vermont

TRAIL COFFEE

AT HOME:
Take 1 packaged coffee ring for each day's coffee in a plastic bag.

IN CAMP:
Boil 2 cups of water and add a coffee ring to soak for a few minutes. Add more water as desired—each ring makes 4 to 6 cups. Wring out used rings and add to trash bag to tote out.

> *Tom Milford*
> *Black Mountain, North Carolina*

GRAND CANYON JAVA

    1 oz. powdered milk
    1 oz. sugar
    ½ oz. powdered coffee
    1 oz. liquid margarine

AT HOME:
Mix dry ingredients together; put liquid margarine in squeeze tube. Package some G.I. heat tabs.

IN CAMP:
Heat 1 cup water over heat tabs and add 1 tablespoon dry ingredients and a squirt of margarine. Heat until all are dissolved, and drink. Provides fat for the diet as well as rich taste.

> *John R. Thybom*

FRUIT TEA

    3 cups boiling water
    3 tablespoons tea *or* 6 tea bags
  ½ cup honey *or* sugar
    4 lemons, juiced *or* 2 cans frozen lemonade
    5 oranges, juiced *or* 1 can frozen orange juice
    1 teaspoon vanilla extract
    3 quarts water

AT HOME:
Steep tea in boiling water. Boil together honey and water about 5 minutes. Add fruit juices, vanilla, and syrup to tea. Mix well and serve hot or cold. Pack in thermos or canteen to drink on the trail, hot or cold.

HERB TEAS

AT HOME:
Package leaves of chamomile, lemon balm, spearmint, peppermint, rosemary, sage, comfrey or basil for hot tea in camp.

IN CAMP:
    1 teaspoon herb leaf, brought from home, or pennyroyal
             found beside mountain trails in the Sierra.
    1 cup boiling water
Steep herb leaves in boiling water for five minutes. Strain, and drink plain or with honey. Good hot or cold.

ROSE HIBISCUS TEA

  1 part hibiscus flowers
  1 part rose hips
  1 part lemon grass
  1 part cinnamon bark
  3 whole cloves

AT HOME:
Mix ingredients and store in a tin for later use. Package in paper bag the amount needed for each outing.

IN CAMP:
Add 2 teaspoons tea mixture to 2 cups boiling water and steep for 5 minutes. Strain, and drink plain, or with honey or lemon. Good cold, too. Makes 2 cups.

SPICED TEA

> 2 cups Tang
> ½ cup instant tea
> 1 package lemonade powder (1 qt.)
> 1½ cups sugar
> 1 teaspoon cinnamon
> ½ teaspoon ground cloves

AT HOME:
Mix all ingredients and store in a jar, or seal in plastic bags, ready for the trail.

IN CAMP:
Add 3 teaspoons tea mixture to each cup of boiling water and stir.

Heather Bryant
Oakland, California

TRAIL SHAKE

> ⅓ cup instant dry milk
> 2 tablespoons powdered nondairy creamer
> 1 tablespoon custard mix
> 1 envelope instant breakfast drink, any flavor.
> 1¼ cups cold water

AT HOME:
Mix milk, creamer, and custard mix together in a plastic bag.

ON THE TRAIL:
Mix ingredients from plastic bag with instant breakfast drink and water in a plastic shaker with a tight lid, and shake vigorously. For extra richness, add malt to taste.

Sister Christine Oleske
O'Neill, Nebraska

INSTANT HOT CHOCOLATE

  1 box (8 quarts) powdered milk
  2 lbs. Nestle's Quik
10 oz. nondairy creamer

AT HOME:
Mix ingredients together and store in a tin. Package in plastic bags the amount needed for each outing (1 or 2 cups per person per day).

IN CAMP:
For each cup of chocolate, pour boiling water over ¼ cup of mixture and stir.

Christine L. Erickson
Black River Falls, Wisconsin

FLAVORING CHOCOLATE

AT HOME:
Package an eyedropper bottle filled with mint or almond extract to go with the trip's chocolate or carob supply.

IN CAMP:
Add a few drops of flavoring to each cup of chocolate or hot carob for new flavor.

Christine Ayars
Pasadena, California

HOT JELL-O DRINK

AT HOME:
Package fruit gelatin (any flavor) for as many meals as desired.

IN CAMP:
    1 2-oz. package fruit gelatin
    3 cups boiling water

Dissolve gelatin in cups of water and drink hot, before dinner in a winter camp.

George Williams
Keokuk, Iowa

ALTERNATIVES:
Postum, Ovaltine, and Tang also make good hot drinks for a winter camp.

CHEAPER-ADE

    1 1-qt. package unsweetened lemon powder
    ½ teaspoon salt
    ¼ teaspoon baking soda
    10 teaspoons sugar

AT HOME:
Mix ingredients together and package in plastic bag.

ON THE TRAIL:
Mix package with 1 quart water and shake until dissolved. Provides a sweat-replacement drink for less money than commercial products.

John D. Wilson, M.D.
Portland, Oregon

Eggs, Cheese, & Yoghurt

EGGS—FRESH

AT HOME:
Package fresh eggs in fiber, plastic, or aluminum egg cartons. Or pack eggs in plastic screw-top jars with rice or cereals to prevent breakage.

Eggs may be broken into plastic bottles and frozen for use on the first or second day. Add lemon juice, herbs, or other seasonings to the eggs, and freeze. Keep cool.

IN CAMP:
Serve scrambled eggs on half a buttered English muffin, topped with a slice of ham or sausage.

✿ DEVILED EGGS

> 2 eggs per person
> 2 tablespoons white wine
> 2 tablespoons mayonnaise
> 1 tablespoon dry mustard
> ½ teaspoon tarragon, basil, *or* parsley

AT HOME:
Boil eggs, cool, slice lengthwise. Mash yolks with seasonings and stuff back into whites. Fold halves together, wrap in plastic wrap, and chill.

ON THE TRAIL:
Eat eggs for lunch the first day with vegetables, fruit-nut breads, lemonade.

✿ EGG SALAD

        4 eggs
        1 tablespoon celery, diced
     1–2 radishes, *or* 1 green onion, diced
        2 tablespoons mayonnaise
        1 teaspoon dry mustard

AT HOME:
Hard-boil eggs, cool, peel, and chop fine. Add chopped vegetables, and seasonings. Mix well, put in plastic screw-top jar, or stuff into a half pita, and wrap in plastic. Chill.

ON THE TRAIL:
Eat egg salad on crackers, or as a sandwich in halves of pita (Arab pocket bread), for first day's lunch.

✿ OMELET

        2 eggs
     2–3 green onions, chopped fine
        1 oz. Swiss cheese, grated
        2 tablespoons sapsago cheese
       ½ green pepper, minced
        2 oz. cream cheese
        2 tablespoons butter
       ½ cup alfalfa sprouts

IN CAMP:
Beat one egg at a time and add to pan with butter. When egg is firm, remove from heat and top with any or all of vegetables and cheeses. Serves two.

❋ EGGS AND PEPPERS

    2 slices bacon
    4 eggs
    2 oz. mild chile peppers, diced
    1 tomato, diced
    1 teaspoon basil leaves
  ¼ teaspoon black pepper *or* paprika
    1 tablespoon parsley, minced

IN CAMP:
Cut bacon in 1″ pieces and fry. Remove bacon and sauté tomato in a small amount of bacon fat or butter. Beat eggs, add peppers, bacon, tomato. Return mixture to pan and cook slowly, lifting edges of egg to permit uncooked portion to run underneath as the omelet cooks. Serves two.

EGGS—FREEZE-DRIED AND DRIED

    2 oz. dried eggs
  ½ teaspoon curry powder *or*
         ½ teaspoon garlic powder
  ½ teaspoon basil, tarragon *or* other herbs
  ½ teaspoon grated sapsago cheese *or*
         other hard cheese
    1 tablespoon powdered milk
      Butter *or* oil

AT HOME:
Mix seasonings with eggs and package in plastic bag.

IN CAMP:
Add water to egg mixture to form a thin paste. Cook slowly in butter or oil until the egg mixture is firm. Serves two.

VARIATION:
Take along packages of freeze-dried instant eggs and add onion

flakes, garlic powder, cheese, alfalfa or bean sprouts along with hot water. Stir, let set a few minutes, and serve.

✿ TRAIL EGGS

>   4 fresh eggs *or* 4 oz. powdered eggs
> ½ bacon bar (1 oz.)
> ½ teaspoon garlic powder
> ⅛ teaspoon salt
> ⅛ teaspoon pepper
>   2 tablespoons butter *or* oil

AT HOME:

Package eggs in cartons, *or* pour powdered egg into plastic bag with bacon bar and seasonings.

IN CAMP:

Beat eggs and pour into buttered pan. Stir in bacon bar and seasonings and cook slowly. If dried eggs are used, add water to powdered egg mixture to form a medium paste. Stir into buttered pan and cook slowly until mixture becomes firm. Serves two.

Grant Fetters
Shelby, Michigan

CHEESE

Cheese is an original and basic travel food—rich in fats and proteins, flavorful, easily combined with grains, pastas, and other starches to provide easy meals for the trail. Cheese has a long history: nomadic Middle Eastern herdsmen 2,000 years ago developed a kind of yoghurt by carrying milk in a container made of a calf's stomach. The enzyme rennin in the calf's stomach caused curdling, and cheese was formed. And cheese may have been made even earlier.

According to Marco Polo, dried milk was prepared by Mongol nomads. As fat rose to the top of a container of milk, it was removed. Then the milk was placed in the sun until the water evaporated and a dried residue remained. The Mongols reconstituted the dried milk as we do—by adding water.

Our grandparents made cottage cheese and clabber from whole milk by setting the milk in the sun until the curd and whey separated. The curd, called "clabber" was eaten for lunch or as a snack at bedtime. To make cottage cheese, the curd was hung to drain in a cheese-cloth bag over a pan until all the whey had drained away. The remaining curd was a dry cottage cheese, which was eaten with salt and pepper as a salad, along with boiled greens or boiled beans. The whey was fed to the chickens or the pigs. Other milk was churned into butter, with a side product—buttermilk—for drinking or baking.

A great variety of cheese is available for cooking and eating on the trail. Do locate a good cheese store and avoid—when possible —the processed cheese foods sold in supermarkets. A good cheese, waxed and hard, will resist mold, heat, and deterioration for weeks, if it is kept cool. In terms of nutrition, flavor, and variety, cheese is an excellent bargain, no matter how expensive it may appear.

Remember that cheese—unlike meat—has no waste. Here are a few cheeses to consider when you are planning the menu for an outing:

AMERICAN CHEDDAR: Can be mild or sharp. Good for cooking, sandwiches, desserts.

BLUE AND BLEU: American, French, or Danish. All varieties resemble Roquefort and are sharp and flavorful. Use in salads, eggs, for desserts, or mix with yoghurt as a sandwich spread or dip.

BRIE: A French cheese, resembling Camembert but sharper in flavor. Has a firm rind and a soft interior; good with fruits for desserts.

CAMEMBERT: A French cheese with a firm rind and soft interior. A good dessert cheese, with crackers and fruits.

CHEDDAR: An English cheese, hard in texture, mild or sharp in flavor. For cooking or desserts, sandwiches or spreads.

CLUB CHEESES: Cheddar types, natural and blended with condiments or wine. Usually come in nut-covered balls, or in crocks.

COTTAGE: A soft-curd, unripened cheese, bland in flavor. Good for salads, cooking, with eggs, or plain, for lunch. Does not keep well.

CREAM: A soft, white, unripened cheese. Use in salads, sandwiches, or with fruits. Does not keep well.

EDAM: A hard Dutch cheese with nutty flavor. Comes in a wax-covered ball. Good for lunch or dessert. Keeps well.

EMMENTHALER: A yellow Swiss cheese with holes; has a nutty flavor. Good for sandwiches and for cooking.

FETA: A soft, white Greek cheese made of goat's milk and cured in brine. Sharp and salty. Good with fruit, in sandwich spreads, or for baking.

GAMMELOST: Hard, brown, strongly flavored Norwegian cheese. Good for lunches and snacks. Keeps well.

GORGONZOLA: Italian blue cheese, similar to Roquefort. Use for salads, desserts, spreads.

GOUDA: A hard Dutch cheese, similar to Edam, but shaped like a flattened ball. Keeps well. Good for lunch or dessert.

GRUYERE: A semihard Swiss used for fondues because it melts easily. Nutty flavor, good for dessert.

JACK OR MONTEREY JACK: A white California cheese. May be hard, semihard, or soft. Has a delicate flavor and is good for cooking, lunches, desserts. The hard type keeps longer than the Teleme, or soft type.

LEYDEN: Dutch cheese similar to Edam, but with caraway seeds. Flavorful; keeps well.

LONGHORN: American Cheddar, cylinder-shaped. Good for cooking, lunches. Keeps well.

MOZZARELLA: Soft, bland, Italian cheese used in pizzas and pasta dishes. Comes in small balls; keeps well if kept cool.

MUENSTER: Semisoft German cheese, good for sandwiches, desserts, with fruits.

NEUFCHATEL: French, soft and similar to cream cheese. Use in salads, sandwiches, desserts. Must be kept cool.

OKA: Canadian, made by Trappist monks, similar to Port du Salut. Semisoft, good for desserts or sandwiches with dark breads.

PARMESAN: Aged, hard Italian cheese, used in Italian dishes, with eggs, soups, stews. Buy in pieces and grate, or buy grated.

PONT L'EVEQUE: Similar to Brie, a French dessert cheese.

PORT DU SALUT: Made by French Trappist monks. Semisoft; keeps well if kept cool. Same uses as Oka, which it resembles.

PROVOLONE: Smoked, hard, pear-shaped, Italian cheese. Slice for lunch or serve with fruit for dessert.

RICOTTA: Fresh, unsalted, Italian cheese, similar to cottage cheese. For cooking or salads. Does not keep well.

ROMANO: Italian sheep's milk cheese similar to Parmesan, a hard cheese for grating into Italian dishes, soup, eggs, stews, vegetables.

ROQUEFORT: The original French blue-veined cheese made of sheep's milk. All other blues are made of cow's milk. A dessert cheese, for salad dressings, eggs, spreads.

SAMSOE: A mild, creamy Danish cheese, good for sandwiches, and cooking.

SAPSAGO: A hard, green Swiss cheese for grating. Comes in a 3-oz. roll and is good in eggs, soups, stews, pasta dishes, or with milder cheeses in spreads. A tart flavor.

STILTON: English blue cheese. For desserts, salad dressings, eggs, and spreads.

SWISS: A mild cheese, good for sandwiches, salads. Same as Emmenthaler, but made in countries other than Switzerland.

TYBO: A mild, nutty-flavored, semihard Danish cheese. Good for lunches, desserts, and cooking. Keeps well.

FOR THE TRAIL:
When possible, purchase whole cheeses in wax coverings. If wedges are purchased, seal them by dipping the cut sides in melted paraffin. It will seal out the air and will peel off easily when the cheese is sliced. Foil or plastic wrap are also good for keeping cheeses on the trail. Keep cheeses cool. Use the softer ones first on an extended trip. If mold appears, scrape it off. It is not dangerous.

✿ YOGHURT

AT HOME:
Fill a quart mayonnaise jar with 5 oz. powdered milk and water. Mix well. Put the jar in a crockpot, fill pot to three-quarters with water. Turn crockpot on high and set a candy thermometer in the milk. When the milk reaches 105°–110°F., add 1 tablespoon plain yoghurt and turn off crockpot heat. Put on lid, cover with a towel for extra warmth. The yoghurt will be ready in 12 to 14 hours. Store in refrigerator.

Pack in screw-top plastic jars for camp.

ON THE TRAIL:
Eat for lunch with fruits, cereals, or vegetables.

✿ ROXANNE'S YOGHURT

> 1¾ cups instant milk powder
> 1 can evaporated milk
> 2 tablespoons plain yoghurt (check yoghurts in market for preservatives and buy purest available)
> Enough water to fill a quart container

AT HOME:
Water should be 110°–120°F. (lukewarm). Mix milks and water, then mix yoghurt with small amount of milk into a soupy mixture. Add the rest of milk, mixing until smooth. Pour in jars, and set in warm water. The water should be level with or just above the yoghurt mixture in the jars.

Set the mixture in the sun and cover with a black plastic sheet. Check water every 3 to 6 hours to be sure it is still warm. At the end of this time, the mixture will solidify. Taste yoghurt. If it isn't sour enough, let it set out of water bath until desired sourness is reached.

Check the yoghurt temperature carefully and keep mixture warm. If it is too cold, it will sour without solidifying; if it is too warm, the yoghurt bacteria will be killed. Keep the yoghurt covered at all times or wild yeasts in the air will drift in and spoil the yoghurt for everything except breadmaking.

FOR THE TRAIL:
Pour in plastic container with screw-top lid, and keep cool on the trail.

IN CAMP:
Eat for lunch with fruits or plain, or with cereals, salads, or fruits for breakfast or dinner.

✿ CHEESE BALLS

½ lb. (1 cup) butter, softened
1 lb. Monterey Jack cheese, grated
¼ cup green onion, chopped fine
1 tablespoon tarragon leaves, crumbled
¼ cup dry white wine
¼ cup walnuts, chopped
1 bunch parsley, minced fine

AT HOME:
Mix softened butter with grated cheese and seasonings and blend well. Mix in wine. Divide cheese into two parts and form each into a roll or ball. Coat with walnuts and parsley. Wrap in foil or plastic and chill until needed.

ON THE TRAIL:
Take along cheese ball or roll for lunch with bread or crackers. Be sure to keep it cool.

✿ CHEESE ROLLS

    8 oz. cream cheese
    ¼ cup mayonnaise
    1 cup chopped ripe olives
    1 tablespoon onion, minced
    ½ teaspoon red *or* black pepper
    ⅛ teaspoon hot pepper sauce
    ½ cup chopped nuts

AT HOME:
Mix softened cheese with all ingredients except nuts. Roll into a ball or rolls, and roll in chopped nuts until cheese is well covered. Wrap in foil or plastic and chill until needed.

ON THE TRAIL:
Take along a roll of cheese to spread on rye bread. Be sure to keep cool.

✿ VERDE SPREAD

    8 oz. cream cheese, softened
    ¼ cup yoghurt
    1 tablespoon chopped chives
    1 tablespoon tarragon leaves
    2 tablespoons parsley, minced (1 tablespoon dried)
    ½ teaspoon chervil leaves
    ¼ teaspoon dill weed
    ⅛ teaspoon black pepper
    ½ teaspoon salt

AT HOME:
Mix softened cheese with yoghurt until smooth. Add other ingredients and mix well.

ON THE TRAIL:
Spread on rye or pumpernickel bread and top with alfalfa sprouts, or serve in half a pita (Arab pocket bread) topped with sprouts, minced green peppers, or pimientos. Be sure to keep cheese cool.

Fried Breads, Sandwiches, & Other Filled Breads

BASIC BREAD

>   3 cups whole wheat flour
>   3 teaspoons baking powder
>   5 tablespoons powdered egg (optional)
> ½ cup powdered milk
> ½ teaspoon salt

AT HOME:
Mix dry ingredients and package in plastic bag. Package any additional ingredients. Recipe yields bread mixture for 3 meals for two.

IN CAMP:
Use recipes as desired:

DROP BISCUITS

>   1 cup flour mixture
> ½ cup water
>   1 tablespoon oil

Mix well and drop by spoonfuls on hot greased griddle or frying pan. Makes 2 to 4 biscuits.

DUMPLINGS

Drop biscuit mixture by spoonfuls into soup or stew. Cook 5 minutes, then cover pot and cook 5 minutes longer. Makes 4 or more dumplings.

BANNOCK

>   1 cup flour mixture
> ¼ cup water
>   1 tablespoon oil

Form mixture into a cake 1″ thick and bake in greased frying pan over low heat until brown. Turn and cook on second side.

SHORTCAKE

Add 1 tablespoon honey or sugar to bannock mixture and cook over low heat until done. Split, butter, and fill with berries or stewed fruit. Top with more fruit.

RICE GRIDDLECAKE

Add ½ cup cooked rice and 1 tablespoon honey to biscuit mixture with enough water to form a batter. Cook on hot greased griddle or frying pan. Makes 3 or 4 cakes. Extras may be used for sandwiches for lunch.

PEANUT BUTTER COOKIES

Add 4 tablespoons peanut butter, 4 tablespoons oats, 4 tablespoons honey, and ¼ cup raisins, dates, or nuts to biscuit mixture. Form into a roll about 2″ in diameter. Cool. Slice cookies about ½″ thick. Cook on lightly greased griddle until brown. Turn and cook on second side.

Melinda Miller
Filer, Idaho

BANNOCK I

1 cup quick oatmeal
1 cup yellow cornmeal
⅓ cup diced almonds
½ teaspoon salt
¼ teaspoon ground ginger
1 teaspoon grated lemon rind
2 cups buttermilk
1 tablespoon molasses
2 eggs
2 tablespoons butter, melted

AT HOME:
Combine dry ingredients in a plastic bag. Pour liquids in separate plastic bottles.

IN CAMP:
Mix ingredients together into a batter. Pour enough batter into a greased hot frying pan to cover bottom to about ¼″ thickness. Cook 10 minutes over medium heat. Turn and cook 5 minutes, or until done. Makes 6 to 8 bannocks. Cut in half, butter, and lay one buttered side over the other. Serve with honey, jam, stewed fruit, or applesauce.

VARIATION:
Make smaller bannocks and top with creamed chicken, turkey, chipped beef.

BANNOCK II

> 1 cup flour
> 1 teaspoon baking powder
> ¼ teaspoon salt
> 2 tablespoons oil

AT HOME:
Package dry ingredients together in a plastic bag. Pour oil into a plastic bottle.

IN CAMP:
Mix dry ingredients with oil and enough water to make a stiff dough. Flatten dough ball into a circle 1″ thick and place in a greased frying pan. Cook over low fire until done, turning once or twice until crust is brown.

> *Barbara Clayton*
> *Dana Point, California*

CHUPPATIES (INDIAN BREAD)

> 1 cup white flour
> 1 cup whole wheat flour
> 1 teaspoon salt
> 2 tablespoons butter, melted
> ½ cup cold water

AT HOME:
Package flour and salt in a plastic bag. Pour butter into a plastic bottle.

IN CAMP:
Mix flour with melted butter and water into a soft dough. Cover and let stand for an hour, then knead well and divide into balls 1½″ to 2″ in diameter. Roll each ball out into a thin circle about 6″ in diameter. Bake on both sides on a hot greased griddle.

FRY-PAN BREAD

- 2 cups flour
- 3 teaspoons baking powder
- 1 teaspoon salt
- 6 tablespoons margarine
- 1 cup berries, any kind

AT HOME:
Sift dry ingredients together. Cut in margarine with pastry cutter or two table knives until well mixed and the consistency of grain. Pour into a plastic bag and store until needed—but not longer than six weeks. Take canned berries or pick along trail.

IN CAMP:
Mix with 1 cup berries and ⅓ cup water into a dough. Form into a cake 1″ thick and the diameter of frying-pan bottom. Cook in a hot greased pan over low heat until brown. Turn, and cook until second side is brown.

Randy Johnson
Newbury Park, California

INDIAN FRY BREAD (*Southwestern Indian*)

      2 cups all-purpose flour
      4 tablespoons powdered milk
      1 teaspoon salt
      1 teaspoon shortening *or* margarine
    ½ cup warm water, or more
      2 cups oil, for frying

AT HOME:
Package dry ingredients in a plastic bag. Pack shortening or
margarine in a screw-top plastic jar, and oil in a plastic bottle.

IN CAMP:
Mix flour with fat and enough water to form a soft dough. Flatten
dough with hands to a round cake about ½" thick. Fry in hot fat
about 1" deep. Turn and brown on second side. Serve with honey
or jam.

VARIATION:
See NAVAJO TACO.

NAVAJO TACO

        2 pieces Indian Fry Bread
    ½–¾ cup chili con carne with beans
        1 4-oz. can diced green chiles
        1 onion, minced
        4 oz. Cheddar cheese, grated

AT HOME:
Freeze chili in plastic carton or package dry chili mix in plastic
bag. Package onion and cheese in separate plastic bags.

IN CAMP:
Fry Indian Fry Bread. Prepare chili and dice onion. On each
piece of fry bread, place half the chili, half the diced green chiles,
minced onion, and grated cheese. Serves two.

CORN TORTILLAS

> 2 cups fine cornmeal
> ½ teaspoon salt
> 1½ cups warm water

AT HOME:
Package cornmeal and salt in a plastic bag.

IN CAMP:
Mix meal and water into a firm, not sticky, dough. Form into balls 1″ to 2″ in diameter and pat out between hands until about 6″ in diameter, or roll out on waxed paper. Cook on a hot griddle until brown on each side. Tortillas burn easily if griddle is too hot. Yield depends on size and thickness.

TORTILLAS

> 1 cup white flour
> 1 cup whole wheat flour
> ½ teaspoon salt
> ⅓ cup oil
> ¾ cup warm water

AT HOME:
Package flour in a plastic bag. Pour oil into a small plastic bottle.

IN CAMP:
Combine flour and salt. Add oil and work with fingers until oil is well distributed. Add water a little at a time until a firm, moist ball is formed. Let set 20 minutes (to permit the flour to glutenate). Break off small pieces of dough and roll or pat into a flat circle about 5″ in diameter. Cook on both sides in an *unoiled* frying pan over moderate heat. Serve with Spiced Lentils (p. 285), or other dishes.

Linnane Blake
Gardner, Colorado

WHOLE WHEAT TORTILLAS

    2 cups whole wheat flour
    ½ teaspoon sea salt
    1 tablespoon corn oil

AT HOME:

Mix flour and salt, then mix in oil. Add water until a soft dough is formed. Add more flour if dough is too sticky. Knead 5 minutes, and form into 1½" balls. Roll out each ball on floured board to ⅛" thickness. Fry in lightly oiled skillet until tortilla bubbles. Turn and brown on second side. Let tortillas cool and package in plastic bag. Yield depends on size and thickness.

IN CAMP:

Roll tortillas around meat or vegetable mixtures for any meal or snack.

Dave Ross
Fort Worth, Texas

✿ ENCHILADAS

    4 tortillas (corn or flour)
    8 oz. ground meat
    1 package enchilada sauce *or* ¼ cup chili sauce
    4 tablespoons chili powder
    1 onion, minced
    1 clove garlic, minced
    4 oz. Cheddar *or* jack cheese, grated
    1 teaspoon salt
    2 tablespoons oil

AT HOME:

Sauté onion in oil, add meat and seasonings and cook until well done. Put one-fourth of the meat on each tortilla, about 1 tablespoon cheese, and roll each into a cylinder. Lay side by side in a baking pan. Cover with sauce and grated cheese and bake in a 350°F. oven for 15 minutes. Cool, fold each enchilada in foil, and freeze.

IN CAMP:
Heat thawed enchiladas and serve for dinner with soup. Serves two.

✿ TOSTADAS

      2 tortillas (corn *or* flour), fried crisply
      1 cup cooked beef, turkey, *or* chicken, chopped
      1 cup cheese, grated (jack, Cheddar, Swiss)
      1 tomato, chopped
      1 green *or* red bell pepper, chopped
      1 onion, minced or sliced thinly
      2 cups lettuce, *or* Chinese cabbage (nappa), finely shredded
      1 avocado, sliced
    ½ cup sour cream
      1 teaspoon Tabasco sauce
      2 tablespoons oil and vinegar dressing, *or* lemon juice

AT HOME:
Package cooked meat, cheese, and tortillas in separate plastic bags. Wash and prepare all vegetables except avocado and tomato. Package sour cream in a screw-top plastic jar.

IN CAMP:
Fry Tortillas (p. 96) and heat meat. Dice tomato and slice avocado. Mix vegetables and add dressing. Place half of meat, vegetables, sour cream, and grated cheese on each tortilla, in that order. Serves two.

PIZZA CRUST

      4 cups flour
      1 tablespoon sugar
      1 teaspoon salt
      1 cake yeast
    ¾ cup warm water
      1 egg, beaten
      2 tablespoons oil

AT HOME:

Sift together dry ingredients. Dissolve yeast in warm water, and add to flour mixture with beaten egg and oil. Mix until dough becomes sticky. Lay out on a well-floured board and knead until elastic. Turn dough ball into an oiled bowl and let rise, covered, about 45 minutes. Punch down, turn over, and let rise a second time, about 1 hour. Divide into four parts and roll each to fit pizza pan or large round tin. Bake for 20 minutes in 425° oven. Makes 4 pizzas, 6 to 8 slices each.

Top crusts with tomato sauce, cheese, anchovies, sausage slices, mushrooms, bacon, or other choices, and brown in broiler. Cool, wrap in foil, and take along whole or cut in wedges for lunch on the trail. Freeze extra crusts.

BOMB-PROOF PIZZA

2½ cups flour (white *or* whole wheat)
1 tablespoon baking powder
1 teaspoon salt
2 packages instant tomato soup
8 oz. cheese, grated or chopped
3 oz. sausage or salami, sliced thinly, *or* canned fish, textured vegetable protein (TVP) *or* other vegetables
3 tablespoons onion flakes
4 cloves garlic, minced
2 tablespoons oregano leaves
4 tablespoons oil

AT HOME:

Package flour with baking powder and salt. Package cheese, sausage or other mixtures separately. Pour oil into plastic bottle.

IN CAMP:

Mix flour with enough water to make a stiff dough. Knead well and flatten thin to fit bottom of frying pan. (Will make 3 or 4 crusts). Mix soup, TVP, and vegetables with seasonings in enough water to make a thick paste. Let stand 10 minutes or until well mixed and vegetables softened. Oil frying pan, place one crust in pan, brown on one side, and turn. Add more oil to frying pan, top crust with sauce, sausage or fish, and cheese. Cover and cook over a low flame until cheese is melted and bottom crust is crisp. Repeat until crusts are cooked and topping mixtures divided among crusts.

Ted Lannan
Lincoln, Nebraska

PANCAKES

> 4 oz. pancake mix
> 1 oz. shredded coconut *or*
> > ½ cup figs, chopped finely *or*
> > 1 teaspoon grated orange or lemon peel *or*
> > ½ cup nuts, chopped fine *or*
> > 2 tablespoons cheese, grated
> 1 package sour cream sauce
> 2 tablespoons oil

AT HOME:
Package pancake mix in a plastic bag. Package any fruit, nuts, or additional foods to be used with pancakes.

IN CAMP:
Mix pancake flour with enough water to make a thin batter. Mix in shredded coconut, figs, dates, nuts, or orange or lemon peel, and pour enough of mixture on griddle to form a pancake about 3″ in diameter. Repeat until all cakes are made. When cakes are bubbly, turn and cook on second side. Serve with butter and syrup, or jam. Or add grated cheese and serve with sour cream and grated lemon peel.

VARIATION:
Make pancake batter with 4 oz. gingerbread mix instead of pancake mix. Serve topped with sweet figs, apples, mixed, or marmalade.

✿ CREPES VIENNA

    5 oz. pancake mix
    3 oz. powdered eggs
    2 oz. powdered milk
    1 cup water
    2 tablespoons oil *or* butter
    2 3-oz. packages cream cheese
    1 can Vienna sausages
    2 tablespoons pickle relish (optional)

AT HOME:
Package dry ingredients together in a plastic bag. Package cheese in a second plastic bag.

IN CAMP:
Mix dry ingredients with water to form a thin batter. Pour 4" to 5" diameter pancakes on oiled griddle or frying pan. Turn when tops are covered with bubbles, and brown second side. Spread each with softened cream cheese mixed with pickle relish. Place a Vienna sausage in the middle and roll into a cylinder. Serves two or three.

✿ SOUR CREAM FOLDOVERS

    4 oz. pancake mix
    2 oz. powdered eggs
    2 oz. powdered milk
    1 cup water
    2 tablespoons oil *or* butter
    1 tablespoon brown sugar
    1 package sour cream mix *or* ½ cup sour cream
    2 peaches, sliced thinly

AT HOME:
Package dry ingredients together in a plastic bag. Package sugar and sour cream in separate bags. Wash peaches, wrap in a paper towel, and package in a plastic bag.

IN CAMP:

Mix together dry ingredients with water. Pour half of mixture into oiled pan for a large pancake. Turn once when top is covered with bubbles, and brown on second side. Spread sour cream on half the pancake. Sprinkle with sugar, add 1 sliced peach, and fold the other pancake half over filling. Repeat for second pancake. Serves two.

VARIATION:

Strawberries, other fresh fruits, or stewed fruits, may be used.

FRENCH TOAST I

    4 1″ thick slices French bread *or* raisin bread
    1 egg, beaten
    2 tablespoons milk powder
   ¼ teaspoon cinnamon
   ¼ teaspoon nutmeg
    2 drops vanilla
    2 tablespoons vegetable oil

AT HOME:

Package bread in plastic bag. Mix milk powder and seasonings and package in a second bag.

IN CAMP:

Mix milk with 1 cup water, vanilla, and the beaten egg. Soak bread slices briefly on each side in the mixture, and fry on a greased hot griddle or frying pan, until brown, 1 or 2 minutes on each side. Serve with butter and marmalade, honey, or jam. Serves two.

VARIATIONS:

1. Serve with cream cheese and jam.
2. Add 1–2 teaspoons maple syrup to batter.

FRENCH TOAST II

    4 slices bread
    2 oz. pancake mix
    1 tablespoon wheat germ
    1 egg, beaten
    2 tablespoons milk powder
    ¼ teaspoon cinnamon
    ¼ teaspoon cloves
    2 tablespoons vegetable oil

AT HOME:
Package seasonings, milk powder, pancake mix and wheat germ in a plastic bag. Package bread in a second bag.

IN CAMP:
Mix together dry ingredients with 1 cup water and add egg. Mix well. Slice bread diagonally and dip in batter, soak about ½ minute on each side. Fry on a hot greased griddle or frying pan until brown, about 1 minute on each side. Serves two.

GUACAMOLE

    2 avocados, very ripe
    3 cloves garlic, minced
    2 tablespoons lemon juice
    1 tomato, diced fine
    ¼ teaspoon salt
  4–5 drops Tabasco sauce, *or* dash of cayenne

AT HOME:
Package avocados and other vegetables whole in plastic bags or boxes.

IN CAMP:
Slice avocados lengthwise, discard seeds, and scoop out meat. Mash and mix with tomato and seasonings and return to the shells, two halves per person. Serve with corn chips or crackers. Serves two.

VARIATION:
Fill tortillas with mixture, roll into a cylinder, and eat.

TOAST WITH GUACAMOLE

　　4 slices whole-grain bread, toasted
　　2 avocados, very ripe
　　2 cloves garlic, minced
　½ teaspoon cayenne
　　1 tomato, chopped fine

AT HOME:
Package bread in plastic bag. Package whole vegetables in another plastic bag.

IN CAMP:
Mash avocado and mix in tomato and seasonings. Spread on toasted bread. Serves two.

VARIATION:
Top mixture with alfalfa sprouts.

SANDWICHES AND SANDWICH SPREADS

AT HOME:
Prepare sandwich spreads, package in plastic bags or boxes. Package nut breads, muffins, or crackers. Or pack spreads into pita, the Arab pocket bread. Other containers for sandwich spreads are:

Half a green or red sweet pepper sliced lengthwise, seeds removed. Fill with a cheese mixture, top with other filled half, and wrap in plastic. Chill, keep cool.

A length of celery 3" or 4" long may be filled with a chosen mixture. Top with a matching length of filled celery stalk. Wrap in plastic and chill.

The wide stems of Chinese (nappa) cabbage may be used in the same way as celery. Shred the green tops to add to *tostadas* or *tacos*. Keeps well.

Toasted English muffins are good topped with a mixture of cream cheese, nuts, and chopped olives, with lemon juice.

Cucumbers, sliced lengthwise, seeds scooped out, may be filled with sandwich spreads.

A few of the many combinations of cheese, fruits, and vegetables, fish and meats, are listed here. Use imagination and develop others for lunch variety on the trail. See "Safety and Perishables" (p. 51) if your sandwiches include mayonnaise, sour cream, tofu, or yoghurt.

Cream cheese, or cream cheese and cottage cheese mixed with sour cream and spread on fruit-nut bread.

Cream cheese, raisins, figs, or dates, and nuts, chopped finely, mixed with lemon juice, mayonnaise, sour cream, or yoghurt.

Cream cheese, minced cucumber, green onion, basil leaves, parsley, sour cream or yoghurt.

Cheddar cheese, grated, mixed with minced onion, dill weed, mayonnaise, or sour cream.

Banana, crushed and mixed with peanut butter and crumbled bacon and spread on date-nut bread.

Salmon or *tuna,* mixed with minced celery, onion, mayonnaise or yoghurt, and spread on rye bread.

Ham or *tongue,* minced with celery, green onions, ginger root, parsley, sour cream or yoghurt, or a mixture of the two.

Grated carrot, raisins, minced ginger root, mayonnaise with dry mustard and lemon juice, in half a pita (Arab pocket bread).

Guacamole may be stuffed into half of a pita, or into half a cucumber topped with other half.

Sauerkraut, well-drained, with dill weed and chopped Vienna sausage may be packed into half a pita. *Or* top sauerkraut with sausage.

Turnips and other crisp root vegetables may be topped with cheese spreads for lunch or snacks.

ON THE TRAIL:
Enjoy choice of sandwiches near a cool stream or snowbank for lemonade or other fruit drink.

✲ CHOPPED CHICKEN LIVERS

2–3 chicken livers
1 medium onion, chopped fine
2 tablespoons chicken fat
2 eggs, hard-boiled

AT HOME:

Cut chicken fat into small pieces and melt in frying pan. When melted, sauté chopped onion 2 or 3 minutes and add livers. Sauté until just done (2 or 3 minutes), pour into a wooden bowl, and chill. When mixture is cold, chop the livers and peeled eggs together until fine and well mixed. Package in a plastic box or jar with screw-top lid. Keep cool.

ON THE TRAIL:

Spread on buttered bread and serve with a dill pickle. Serves two. Or, fill pita bread pockets with mixture, top with diced dill pickles. Serves two.

VARIATION:

4 or 5 ounces liver sautéed and chilled. Chop with onion, celery, and mix with 1 tablespoon mayonnaise and 1 tablespoon sour cream, salt, and pepper to taste.

✲ SAUSAGE AND PINEAPPLE SPREAD

1 3-oz. package cream cheese
1 4" smoked sausage
1 3" wedge fresh pineapple
1 green onion, minced
1 tablespoon ginger root, minced or grated
½ teaspoon lime juice
¼ teaspoon garlic powder

AT HOME:

Chop pineapple and sausage fine. Add seasonings and mix with softened cheese. Package in plastic container and chill.

ON THE TRAIL:
Fill halves of pita (Arab pocket bread) with the spread and top
with a sprig of Chinese parsley (coriander leaves). Serves two.

❀ TUNA SPREAD

1 6½-oz. can tuna
1 6-oz. jar marinated artichoke hearts
1 2¼-oz. can chopped ripe olives
1 small onion, minced
1 small cucumber, minced
2 tablespoons lemon juice
½ teaspoon basil leaves
½ teaspoon oregano leaves

AT HOME:
Mix together all ingredients and store in a plastic jar until needed.
Keep cool.

ON THE TRAIL:
Fill halves of pita (Arab pocket bread) with the mixture. Serves
four.

VARIATION:
Substitute chopped ham or bacon and grated cheese for tuna. Top
stuffed pita halves with wedges of tomato.

❀ TOFU SPREAD

1 8-oz. package tofu
1 small can clams or tuna
1 package onion soup mix
2 green onions, minced
1 clove garlic, minced
2 tablespoons parsley flakes *or* fresh, minced
1 tablespoon dry mustard

AT HOME:
Mash tofu and mix all ingredients well. Place in plastic container and store in refrigerator.

ON THE TRAIL:
Spread on bread, stuff into half a pita (Arab pocket bread), or use as a dip with crisp celery, turnip rounds, or other crisp vegetables. Serves four.

✿ SUSHI

Sushi is a dish of raw, smoked or pickled fish and vegetables wrapped in cold, seasoned rice, eaten for lunch and snacks by the Japanese. The rice should be sticky, so ordinary (not instant) rice should be used:

        1 cup rice
        2 tablespoons wine vinegar *or* rice vinegar
    1¼ cups water
        4 8-in. sheets kelp

AT HOME:
Add rice to water, cover, and bring to a boil. Turn off heat and let stand 3 minutes. Return to medium heat and cook 15 minutes. Lower heat and cook 10 minutes longer.

Add 1 or 2 tablespoons wine or rice vinegar to the rice. Make balls of rice with bits of ham, shrimp, pickled herring, raw fish, smoked salmon, egg yolks, mushrooms, onions, celery, or other vegetables inside. Wrap in a piece of kelp (from Oriental stores), and package in plastic bags, or place in a small box, Japanese-style.

ON THE TRAIL:
Keep sushi cool and eat for lunch or snack. Raw salmon or tuna are best if raw fish is used. Whether it is prepared at home or from fish caught near camp, eat it the day it is prepared.

VARIATION:
A Turkish variety may be made by mixing raisins and pine nuts with rice and folding in steamed grape leaves.

Crackers,
Flat Breads,
& Muffins

CHEESE AND DILL CRACKERS

    1 cup self-rising flour
    ½ cup quick oats
    ½ cup wheat germ
    ⅓ cup sesame seeds
  2–3 tablespoons dill weed
    1 tablespoon onion flakes
    ½ cup sharp Cheddar cheese, grated
    1 teaspoon salt
    ¾ cup water

AT HOME:
Mix dry ingredients together, add cheese and oil. Blend thoroughly. Add water and mix until a thick dough is formed. Spread the dough on a greased baking sheet, about ⅛" to ¼" thick. With a table knife, score lengthwise and crosswise in 1" or 1½" squares. Bake in a 350° oven about 45 minutes. Let dry in warm oven for 2 or 3 hours. Cool; store in covered tins.

    Package several squares in plastic bags for each hiker's snack on the trail.

Inez Frink
Tallahassee, Florida

COBBLESTONE CRACKERS

    1 cup flour
    1 cup bran
    ½ cup buttermilk
    2 tablespoons butter
    1 teaspoon salt

AT HOME:
Mix dry ingredients and cut in butter with table knives or fingers

until well mixed and the particles are the size of fine grains. Add milk gradually until a stiff dough is formed. Knead 4 or 5 minutes on a floured board and divide into 12 balls. Roll each ball between lightly floured sheets of waxed paper until about ⅛″ thin and 6″ in diameter. Remove paper and bake crackers about 2 minutes on a hot ungreased griddle. Turn and bake on second side. Place on baking sheet and bake in a 250°F. oven for 30 minutes. Turn off oven and leave crackers to dry as oven cools. Store in a tin until needed. Pack in plastic bags for the trail.

VARIATION:
Substitute whole wheat flour or cornmeal for half the flour. Add garlic powder, dill weed, chili powder or Parmesan cheese, or ½ teaspoon cumin or coriander.

Dan Hardt
San Diego, California

GRAHAM CRACKERS

    2 cups graham flour
    1 cup white flour
    1 teaspoon baking powder
    ½ teaspoon baking soda
    ¼ teaspoon salt
    ½ cup oil
    ¾ cup brown sugar
    ¼ cup milk
    1 teaspoon vanilla

AT HOME:
Sift together dry ingredients. Cream oil and sugar, add milk and vanilla. Mix in flour gradually, beating well after each addition. Chill dough several hours until stiff. Divide into thirds and roll each portion on a floured board to a ⅛″ thick rectangle. Score dough lengthwise and crosswise in 2″ or 3″ squares, or any other desired size. Mark squares with tines of a fork. Place on greased baking sheets and bake in a 350°F. oven 10 to 12 minutes, or until crisp. Cool, store in tins in a cool place. Makes about 36 crackers. Pack in plastic bags for the trail.

VARIATION:
Sprinkle with 1 tablespoon coarse salt *or* 2 tablespoons caraway, poppy, or sesame seeds before baking.

PACKER'S CRACKERS

2 cups whole wheat flour *or* part white flour
1 cup soy flour
1 cup wheat germ
4 cups oatmeal
1 cup sesame seeds
4 teaspoons baking powder
4 teaspoons salt
4 teaspoons sugar
2 teaspoons baking soda
¾ cup corn oil
2 cups buttermilk

AT HOME:
Sift flour into a large mixing bowl and mix in other dry ingredients. Add corn oil and buttermilk and mix thoroughly. Roll dough in a ball and divide into four parts. With floured hands, pat each part into a rectangle on a floured board. Roll out to about 1/16" thickness and press broken edges together with fingers. With a knife, score dough lengthwise and crosswise into crackers 1½" square. Lift crackers with a spatula and place on a baking sheet in rows. Prick each with tines of a fork to release moisture. Bake in a 350°F. oven 15 minutes or until brown. Turn off oven and let crackers dry for 30 to 45 minutes. Cool, store in tins. Dough may be frozen for later use. Makes approximately 150 crackers.

FOR CAMP AND TRAIL:
Pack crackers in stacks of six to a plastic bag, to eat on trail or with soup in camp.

Jim and Marge Gray
Escondido, California

WHOLE WHEAT CRACKERS

        2 cups whole wheat flour
    1½ teaspoons salt
        5 tablespoons oil
    ½ cup water
        2 tablespoons sesame seeds

AT HOME:

Mix all ingredients together thoroughly. Add enough water to form a firm dough. Knead until smooth, 10 to 12 times. Divide dough into four parts and roll out each part on a floured board into a rectangle about ⅛" thick. With a knife, score lengthwise and crosswise into crackers 2" to 3" square or larger, as desired. Sprinkle with sesame seeds. Place on greased baking sheets and bake in a 425°F. oven 10 minutes. Cool, and store in closed tins in a cool place. Makes about 24 crackers. Pack in plastic bags for the trail.

VARIATION:

Make round crackers with biscuit cutter or small juice can. Sprinkle with poppy seeds, caraway seeds, or other seeds for different flavors.

RYE CRACKERS

        1 cup rye flour
        1 cup white flour
    ½ teaspoon salt
    ½ cup water
        5 tablespoons oil
        2 tablespoons caraway or poppy seeds

AT HOME:

Mix all ingredients together thoroughly; add more water if needed to make a stiff dough. Knead 10 or 12 times. Divide into four parts and roll out each part on a floured board into a rectangle about ⅛" thick. With a knife, score dough lengthwise and crosswise into crackers 2" or 3" square, or any desired size. Sprinkle with caraway or poppy seeds. Place on greased baking sheet and bake in a 425°F. oven 10 minutes. Cool, store in tins in a cool place. Makes about 24 crackers. Pack in plastic bags for the trail.

VARIATION:
Sprinkle with 2 tablespoons grated hard cheese or with 1 table-spoon sea salt before baking.

RYE PRETZELS

        1 package active dry yeast
    1½ cups warm water
        1 tablespoon malted milk powder
        1 tablespoon molasses
        1 teaspoon salt
    4–4¾ cups rye flour
        1 tablespoon caraway seeds
    2–3 tablespoons coarse salt

AT HOME:
Dissolve yeast in warm water. Add malted milk powder, molasses, and salt. Stir in rye flour and caraway seeds. The dough will be stiff. Knead until smooth, about 5 minutes. Roll into a long rope and cut into 12 portions. Roll each rope to 15″ length. Sprinkle board with coarse salt and roll ropes in salt. Form into pretzels, figure-eight style, and pinch ends together in center. Moisten slightly with water. Lay on greased baking sheets and bake in a 425°F. oven for 20 minutes. Cool, store in tins in a cool place. Makes 24 pretzels. Pack in plastic bags for the trail.

ROMAN RUSK

        1 cup flour
    ½ cup honey

AT HOME:
Mix flour and honey. Spread batter in thin biscuits on a baking sheet. Bake in a 350°F. oven until brown, about 15 minutes.

Cool, store in tins in a cool place. Pack in plastic bags for the trail.

Neal D. Fortin
Huntington Woods, Michigan

Rusk was used first by the Roman legions as marching rations. As the Roman Empire spread, so did the consumption of rusk. When you taste it, you will understand why the Roman Empire was so successful.

FLAT BREAD

2 cups warm water
1 tablespoon salt
1 tablespoon vegetable oil
1 tablespoon honey
3 cups whole wheat flour
¼ cup sesame seeds *or* 3 tablespoons chopped onions,
            dill weed, *or* mixed herbs (thyme, basil, etc.)

AT HOME:
Pour warm water into mixing bowl and add salt, oil, and honey. Stir until dissolved. Add enough flour to make a sticky dough. Into the dough, knead seeds or herbs to taste. Or divide the dough and add a different seasoning to each portion. Roll dough out into a circle or rectangle ¼" thick. Cut into rounds or squares. Bake on greased baking sheet in a 350°F. oven for 7 minutes for a breadlike texture, or 10 minutes for crisp crackers. Cool, store in tins in a cool place.

ON THE `TRAIL:
Mix the ingredients and cook in a skillet.

Kaaren Wiken
Mukwonago, Wisconsin

MOLASSES HARDTACK

        1 teaspoon baking soda
       ⅔ cup cold water
        2 eggs
        2 cups molasses
       ⅔ cup shortening, melted
        1 teaspoon ginger
      5½ cups whole wheat flour
        1 cup raisins

AT HOME:
Dissolve baking soda in cold water. Beat eggs, molasses, and melted shortening together. Add ginger and soda in water. Mix well. Add flour and raisins. Mixture should be stiff. Roll 1 heaping tablespoon of dough in flour until it is 5″ long. Lay on a greased baking sheet and flatten with a spatula. Roll and flatten rest of dough in a similar manner. Bake in a 350°F. oven about 15 minutes. Makes 18 or 20 biscuits. Store in tins in a cool place.

FOR THE TRAIL:
Place biscuits in plastic bags for snacks.

Janis Kay
Manchester, Connecticut

HUDSON BAY BREAD

        2 cups sugar
       ⅓ cup honey
       ⅓ cup dark Karo syrup
        2 cups margarine
      9½ cups rolled oats
        1 cup sliced almonds
        1 cup shredded coconut

AT HOME:
Cream sugar, honey, syrup, and margarine together. Mix in rolled

oats, almonds, and coconut. Spread on a greased baking pan about ½" thick. Bake in a 350°F. oven until light brown, about 18 minutes. Cool for 4 hours before cutting into squares. Wrap in plastic, store in a cool place.

ON THE TRAIL:
A good snack that keeps well.

> *Staff of*
> *Charles L. Sommers BSA Canoe Base*
> *Ely, Minnesota*

LOGAN BREAD

        10 cups whole wheat flour
         2 teaspoons baking powder
        ¾ cup powdered milk
         1 tablespoon salt
         2 teaspoons nutmeg
         1 tablespoon coriander
      1¼ cups honey
      1½ cups blackstrap molasses
      1¾ cups brown sugar
         1 quart water
      1½ cups vegetable oil
         3 cups nuts, chopped—any kind or mixture

AT HOME:
Sift dry ingredients together. Stir honey, molasses and sugar into water until dissolved. Add oil. Mix in dry ingredients gradually. Add nuts. Pour into greased baking pans 9" x 13" x 2" and bake in a 300°F. oven for 1 hour. Cool, cut into 2" squares, and return to a 140°F. oven to dry. Or let dry at room temperature overnight. Wrap squares in foil or plastic and store in a cool place.

ON THE TRAIL:
Good for any meal. This bread keeps well.

LOGAN BREAD, LAURA'S WAY

 2 cups rye flour
 1 cup whole wheat flour
 ¾ cup wheat germ
 ½ cup powdered milk
 ¼ cup brown sugar
 ½ cup walnuts *or* pecans
 ½ cup raisins
 ½ cup dried peaches, apricots, *or* dates, chopped
 2 tablespoons peanut oil
 ½ cup honey
 ¼ cup molasses
 ¼ cup sorghum syrup *or* maple syrup
 6 eggs

AT HOME:
Sift together dry ingredients and mix in sugar, nuts, raisins, and dried fruits. Beat in peanut oil, honey, molasses, and eggs. Mixture should be heavier than bread dough. Press into greased baking pans about 1″ deep. Bake in a 275°F. oven for 2 hours, or until done. This bread burns easily and may be baked at lower temperature. Cool, cut into squares, and wrap in plastic. Store in a cool place.

ON THE TRAIL:
A nutritious fruit-nut bread for snacks or meals.

Laura Waterman
East Corinth, Vermont

OATCAKES

 4 cups rolled oats
 1 cup whole wheat flour
 1 teaspoon salt
 1 teaspoon baking soda
 3 tablespoons margarine
 1 cup boiling water

AT HOME:
Sift together dry ingredients. Cut in margarine with two knives. Add water gradually, mixing while pouring, until mixture is cohesive but not too wet. Roll out on a floured board until very thin, 1/8″ or less. Cut into 2″ squares and bake on baking sheets in a 375°F. oven, turning once, for 20 to 35 minutes, or until lightly browned. Cool, pack in tins, and store in a cool place. Pack in plastic bags for the trail.

Linda Rimel
Eugene, Oregon

TRAIL BREAD

2½ cups whole wheat flour
1 cup white flour
2 teaspoons salt
2 teaspoons sugar
1½ teaspoons baking powder
1½ cups milk
2 tablespoons butter
5 tablespoons honey

AT HOME:
Sift dry ingredients together. Heat milk with butter and honey. Add milk mixture to flour mixture and knead until dough is formed but not sticky. Shape into flat loaves ½″ to ¾″ thick, square or round. Place on greased baking sheet. Score for easy breaking on the trail. Coat lightly with oil and sprinkle lightly with flour. Bake in a 450°F. oven for 15 minutes. Do not overcook. Cool, store in plastic bags, and refrigerate. Will keep several months if frozen.

ON THE TRAIL:
Eat with cheese and meat for lunch.

John Steingraeber
Grand Rapids, Michigan

TRAIL BREAD, GREG'S WAY

   1 cup whole wheat flour
   ½ cup wheat germ
   ½ cup powdered milk
   1 cup soy flour
   1 teaspoon salt
   4 large eggs
   ½ cup vegetable oil
   ½ cup molasses
   1 teaspoon vanilla
   1 cup raisins
   1 cup dates *or* figs, chopped

AT HOME:
Sift together all dry ingredients. Beat eggs lightly and mix with oil, molasses, and vanilla. Mix in dry ingredients and beat until well mixed. Stir in raisins and dates or figs. The batter will be stiff. Spread in a greased 8″ or 11″ square baking pan. Bake in a 225°F. oven for 1½ hours. Turn off oven and let bread cool. Cut in squares and wrap each in plastic. Store in freezer.

ON THE TRAIL:
Eat for lunch or snacks.

Greg Bicho
Neenah, Wisconsin

WHITE MOUNTAIN SURVIVAL BREAD

          2 cups rolled oatmeal
          3 cups flour
          1 cup powdered milk
          1 tablespoon salt
          1 cup wheat germ
          ½ cup sesame seeds
          ½ cup sunflower seeds (chop in blender)
          4 eggs
          ¾ cup peanut butter
          8 oz. cream cheese, softened
          2 cups dates, chopped
          2 cups applesauce
       1¼ cups water

AT HOME:
Mix together dry ingredients. Stir in eggs, peanut butter, and softened cream cheese. Heat dates in water to soften, and add with applesauce to the mixture. Mix well. Spread ½″ thick in shallow baking pans. Bake in a 350°F. oven for 25 minutes. Turn off oven and let dry for 1 hour. Cut in squares or rectangles. Wrap in plastic and store in a cool place.

ON THE TRAIL:
Eat for lunch or snacks.

Kathryn S. Beij
Ashland, New Hampshire

BRAN MUFFINS

       1½ cups bran
          1 cup whole wheat flour
          1 teaspoon baking soda
          1 teaspoon baking powder
          1 teaspoon salt
          ½ cup raisins
          1 egg, beaten
          ½ cup blackstrap molasses
          2 tablespoons oil
          ¾ cup milk

AT HOME:

Mix together dry ingredients and raisins. Beat egg and stir in molasses, oil, and milk. Add to dry ingredients and mix until thoroughly blended. Bake in greased muffin tins in a 400°F. oven 15 minutes, or until done. Makes 12 muffins. Cool, wrap in foil or plastic, and freeze.

IN CAMP:

Heat for breakfast, or eat cold for lunch or dinner.

CARROT BRAN MUFFINS

$1\frac{1}{2}$ cups whole wheat flour
1 teaspoon salt
$1\frac{1}{2}$ teaspoons baking soda
$1\frac{1}{2}$ cups bran
1 tablespoon cinnamon
2 eggs, beaten
$\frac{1}{4}$ cup vegetable oil
2 teaspoons vinegar
$1\frac{1}{2}$ cups milk
$\frac{1}{4}$ cup blackstrap molasses
$\frac{1}{3}$ cup honey
1 cup carrots, grated
$\frac{1}{2}$ cup raisins *and/or* nuts, chopped

AT HOME:

Mix flour and other dry ingredients together. Beat eggs, stir in oil, vinegar, milk, molasses, honey, carrots, and raisins or nuts. Beat well and combine with dry ingredients. Mix but do not beat. Pour into greased muffin tins until each is two-thirds full. Bake in a 375°F. oven for 20 minutes. Makes 24 muffins. Cool, wrap in foil or plastic, and freeze.

IN CAMP:

Heat for breakfast, or eat cold with lunch or dinner.

Thane Riordan
Eugene, Oregon

FRESNO BRAN MUFFINS

  1 cup flour
  1 tablespoon baking powder
  ½ teaspoon cinnamon
  ½ teaspoon salt
  1 cup whole bran
  ¾ cup milk
  2 tablespoons shortening
  ⅓ cup sugar
  1 egg, well beaten
  1 cup dried figs, chopped

AT HOME:
Sift flour with baking powder, cinnamon, and salt. Soak bran in milk for 5 minutes. Cream shortening with sugar. Add egg/bran mixture, and figs. Stir in flour and blend well. Fill greased muffin pans two-thirds full. Sprinkle tops with sugar. Bake in a 375°F. oven for 25 minutes. Makes 12 muffins. Cool, wrap in foil and freeze.

IN CAMP:
Warm muffins in foil over hot-water pot.

> *Dodie Sway*
> *Western Research Kitchens*
> *Los Angeles, California*

MILLET APPLE MUFFINS

  1½ cups unbleached flour
  3 teaspoons baking powder
  ¾ teaspoon salt
  3 tablespoons brown sugar
  1 teaspoon cinnamon
  ½ teaspoon allspice
  2 eggs
  ½ cup milk
  3 tablespoons butter, softened
  ⅓ cup apple, grated
  ½ cup cooked millet

AT HOME:
Mix together dry ingredients. Beat eggs and stir in milk, butter, apple, and millet. Combine with dry ingredients and pour into greased muffin tins, two-thirds full. Bake in a 400°F. oven for 30 minutes. Makes 12 or 14 muffins. Cool, wrap in foil, and freeze.

IN CAMP:
Heat, or eat cold for breakfast or lunch.

RICE AND RAISIN MUFFINS

1½ cups whole wheat flour
 3 teaspoons baking powder
½ teaspoon salt
½ teaspoon nutmeg
⅓ cup vegetable oil
⅔ cup water
¼ cup honey
½ cup raisins
 2 eggs, beaten
½ cup cooked rice

AT HOME:
Mix together dry ingredients. Heat oil, water, honey, and raisins for 5 minutes. Beat eggs and mix with rice. Combine all ingredients and pour into greased muffin tins, about two-thirds full. Bake in a 400°F. oven for 25 minutes. Makes 12 muffins. Cool, wrap in foil or plastic, and freeze.

IN CAMP:
Heat for breakfast, or eat for lunch and dinner.

SOY MUFFINS

½ cup soy flour
1½ cups white flour
4 teaspoons baking powder
½ teaspoon salt
1 egg
¼ cup blackstrap molasses
1 cup milk
¼ cup oil

AT HOME:
Sift dry ingredients together. Beat egg, mix in molasses, milk, and oil. Combine with dry ingredients and pour into muffin tins, two-thirds full. Bake 20 or 25 minutes in a 425°F. oven. Cool, wrap in foil or plastic, and freeze.

IN CAMP:
Heat for breakfast. Eat for lunch with cheese.

WHEAT BERRY MUFFINS

1 cup whole wheat flour
½ cup white flour
3 teaspoons baking powder
½ teaspoon salt
2 eggs, beaten
⅔ cup milk
⅓ cup oil
¼ cup honey
⅔ cup cooked wheat berries

AT HOME:
Sift together dry ingredients. Beat eggs, add milk, oil, and honey. Combine with dry ingredients and wheat berries. Pour batter into greased muffin tins, about two-thirds full. Bake in a 400°F. oven for 25 minutes. Makes 12 muffins. Cool, wrap in foil or plastic, and freeze.

IN CAMP:
Heat for breakfast. Eat with cheese for lunch, or buttered for dinner, with stews and soups.

Yeast Breads, Fruit Breads, & Cakes

ARAB BREAD (KHUBIS, PITA)

Arab bread, or pita, is also called pocket bread. It puffs up in baking and collapses later. Sliced open, it reveals a pocket that may be filled with meats, vegetables, cheese spreads, fruit mixtures, sprouts, or other foods. Slice across the bread to form two half-pockets, or slice at the edge to provide a whole pocket for either hot or cold fillings. Pita may be made at home, or purchased in some supermarkets, ethnic groceries, or natural-food stores.

ARAB BREAD (KHUBIS, PITA)

     5 lbs. all-purpose flour
 1/4 cup sugar
     2 tablespoons salt
     1 package dry yeast
 1/2 cup warm water
     2 tablespoons olive oil

AT HOME:
Sift together flour, sugar, and salt. Dissolve yeast in warm water until bubbly, and add to flour. Knead 5 to 10 minutes. Cover dough and let stand 5 minutes. Spread oil on dough and mixing pan, cover, and let rise in warm place for 3 hours. Divide dough into 24 equal parts, forming each part into a ball. Let rest for 30 minutes. Roll out each ball on a floured board into a round 7" in diameter and about 3/8" thick. Let rest, covered, 1 hour. Bake on ungreased baking sheets in the *bottom* of a 500°–550° oven 5 to 6 minutes, or until brown on the bottom. Put under broiler 1 minute until tops are browned. Makes 24.

SOURDOUGH STARTER

> 1 tablespoon yeast
> ¼ cup warm water
> 1 teaspoon sugar
> 2 cups flour
> 1⅔ cups warm water
> 1 cup flour

AT HOME:
Dissolve yeast in warm water with sugar and let it proof for 5 minutes. Beat in 2 cups flour and warm water, and let mixture ferment, covered, at room temperature for 4 days, stirring once daily. On the last day, stir in 1 cup flour and let mixture ferment 1 more day.

Store in crock or glass container. Stir at least once a week if not used. When mixture is used, add 1 cup flour for each cup of starter removed.

Starter may be kept in freezer until needed. Add enough flour to make dough and knead into a ball. Wrap in plastic and freeze. To use, thaw and revive with warm water.

ON THE TRAIL:
Take along in a screw-top plastic jar.

IN CAMP:
Form biscuits of the dough and bake; pat out a flat loaf, bannock-style, and bake in a greased frying pan. Or thin the dough with milk and make pancakes.

BAGELS

> 4 cups flour
> 2 packages dry active yeast
> 1 cup soy flour (optional)
> 2 cups warm water
> ¼ cup honey
> 2 teaspoons salt
> 3 tablespoons oil
> 4 eggs, beaten
> 1 cup powdered milk

AT HOME:

Mix yeast with 1 cup flour and 1 cup warm water. Mix in honey, salt, oil, and beaten eggs, and let stand for 5 minutes. Dissolve powdered milk in second cup of warm water and pour into the mixture. Add enough flour to make a batter but not stiff as dough. Let stand 5 to 15 minutes in a warm place. Add enough flour to form a dough, turn out on a floured board and knead, working in enough flour to make a stiff dough. Place dough in an oiled bowl, covered, and let rise in a warm place for 30 minutes. Punch dough down. Divide in half; then divide each half into 12 equal pieces. Roll each piece into a rope 6" to 8" long. Pinch ends together and continue with each rope until 12 bagels are formed. Punch down remaining dough and let stand.

Boil water in a 2- or 3-gallon pot, large enough to boil 12 bagels. Place bagels in water mixed with 1 tablespoon sugar or 1 table-spoon cornmeal. Flip bagels with a slotted spoon after 2 minutes, or when they float to the top. After 2 minutes on each side, remove bagels and drain on baking sheets in a hot oven until tops are dry. Flip onto greased baking sheets and bake 20 to 30 minutes in a 400°F. oven until brown. Cool, place in plastic bags, and store in a cool place. Makes 24 bagels.

ON THE TRAIL:

Take along bagels for lunch with cheese spreads, traditional cream cheese and lox, or for soup. Bagels should be eaten fresh; they become hard after a day or two. Chop hard bagels into soup.

BAGELS, PAUL'S WAY

 5 lbs. (10 cups) whole wheat flour
 1/4 cup yeast
 3 pints warm water
 1/2–1 cup oil
 3/4 cup honey *or* molasses
 2 tablespoons salt
 1 cup finely ground cornmeal
 1/4 cup poppy seeds *or* sesame seeds

AT HOME:

Mix 5 cups flour and half of yeast in a 3-gallon mixing bowl. Add water and mix thoroughly. Add oil, honey, salt, and mix again. Add 3 cups flour. Use remaining flour to flour board, or counter. Turn dough on floured surface and knead 10 minutes. Add flour to board as needed. Place in greased bowl and let rise, covered, in a warm place until it is doubled in size. Punch down dough; divide into three equal parts. Roll out each part into an oblong shape and chop into 12 equal pieces. Roll out each piece to 6" or 8" long, place ends together overlapping about 1", and press firmly together. Turn each bagel in cornmeal and drop into boiling water 2 minutes. Remove to greased cookie sheet, press in poppy or sesame seeds on each side, and dry under broiler for 2 minutes. Bake for 30 minutes in a 400°F. oven. Switch baking tins on shelves after 15 minutes so all will bake evenly. Makes 36 bagels. Cool, store in plastic bags or tins.

ON THE TRAIL:
Enjoy with cheese or with soups, or with traditional lox and cream cheese.

BOB'S BAGELS

        2 packages dry active yeast
4¼–5 cups sifted flour
    1¼ cups lukewarm water
        3 tablespoons sugar
        1 teaspoon salt

AT HOME:
Combine yeast and half the flour in a mixing bowl. Combine water, sugar, salt, and add to flour. Beat for 3 minutes at low speed, then 3 minutes at high speed with electric mixer. Beat by hand, mixing in enough flour to make a moderately stiff dough. Turn onto floured board and knead 10 minutes. Cover, let rest 5 minutes. Divide into 12 portions and shape into smooth balls. Punch holes in balls and form into rings. Cover, let rise 20 minutes. Add 1 tablespoon sugar or salt to 1 gallon water and bring to a boil. Reduce to simmer and boil bagels, 3 or 4 at a time, for 2 minutes, turning once. Drain, bake on greased baking sheet in a 375°F. oven for 30 to 35 minutes. Cool, place in plastic bags or tins. Makes 12 bagels.

VARIATION:
Use whole wheat flour. The bagels will be smaller and heavier.
Use minced onion, oregano, basil, marjoram, or savory.

Jay M. Gregg
Stillwater, Oklahoma

RAISED OVEN DONUTS

      1½ cups milk
       4 tablespoons sugar
       2 teaspoons salt
       2 teaspoons nutmeg
       ½ teaspoon cinnamon
       ⅓ cup oil
       2 eggs, beaten
       2 packages dry active yeast
       4 tablespoons warm water
     4¾ cups flour, sifted

AT HOME:
Scald milk and add sugar, salt, spices, and oil to milk in a large
mixing bowl. Cool to lukewarm. Add beaten eggs. Soften yeast in
warm water until bubbly, about 5 minutes. Add to milk and
beaten eggs. Beat in flour until a dough is formed. Cover and let
stand in a warm place until dough has doubled in bulk, about 1
hour. Turn dough onto a floured board, turning two or three
times to shape into a soft ball. Roll out lightly to about ½" thick.
Cut with a 3" donut cutter and place rings 2" apart on a greased
baking sheet. Place centers between donuts. Bake in a 425°F. oven
for 10 minutes. Cool, store in a covered tin in a cool place. Makes
2½ to 3 dozen donuts.

ENGLISH MUFFINS

    1 package dry yeast
    2 tablespoons warm water
    1 cup water
    ½ cup milk, scalded and cooled
    2 teaspoons sugar
    1 teaspoon salt
    4 cups white flour
    3 tablespoons butter, melted

AT HOME:
Mix yeast with warm water and a pinch of sugar. Mix water, milk, sugar, and salt. When yeast becomes bubbly, add to milk mixture. Beat in 2 cups of flour. Cover bowl and let batter rise in a warm place for about 2 hours, or until it has risen and collapsed. Beat in butter and enough flour to make a thick batter.

Prepare rings about 3″ in diameter from small tin cans. Grease, and place on a board dusted with flour and cornmeal. Pour batter to a depth of ½″ into each ring. Let rise until doubled in bulk. Move muffins with a spatula to a hot greased griddle and cook 5 minutes on each side. Cool, wrap in plastic, and freeze.

Muffin rings may be purchased in kitchen supply stores.

VARIATION:
Add enough flour to the collapsed batter sponge to make a soft dough. Roll to ½″ thickness and cut out rounds with a 3″ diameter metal ring. Place on greased baking sheet, dust with cornmeal, and let rise until double in size. Cook on hot greased griddle 5 minutes on each side. Cool, wrap in plastic, and freeze.

IN CAMP:
Top toasted halves with poached eggs, ham, or cheese for breakfast.

OAT AND FIG BREAD

> 1 package active dry yeast
> ½ cup warm water
> ½ cup quick oats, uncooked
> ½ cup boiling water
> 3 tablespoons shortening
> 1 teaspoon salt
> ½ cup molasses
> 1 egg, beaten
> 2½ cups flour
> ⅔ cup figs, chopped finely

AT HOME:
Mix yeast in warm water and let stand until bubbly, about 10 minutes. Combine oats, boiling water, shortening and salt. Add molasses, let cool to lukewarm. Mix in yeast and beaten egg. Add flour gradually to make a stiff dough. Turn onto floured board and knead about 5 minutes. Return dough to greased bowl and cover. Let stand in a warm place until double in size, about 1 hour. Roll out on floured board to about ½″ thickness and spread figs over dough. Roll up dough and knead lightly to press out air bubbles. Cover and let stand in bowl 5 minutes. Fold ends under and form into a loaf. Place in a greased 9″ x 5″ loaf pan. Brush oil over top and sprinkle with oats. Let stand until double, about 1 hour. Bake in a 350°F. oven for 1 hour, or until done. If top browns too quickly, cover loosely with foil during the last 20 minutes of baking. Cool, store in plastic bag in freezer.

ON THE TRAIL:
Slice, toast, and butter for breakfast, or make sandwiches of cheese or spreads.

ORANGE RYE BREAD

>   2 packages active yeast
>   2¾ cups warm water
>   ½ cup dark brown sugar
>   4 tablespoons salt
>   3 tablespoons butter, softened
>   3 tablespoons grated orange rind
>   3¾ cups unsifted rye flour
> 5½–6½ cups unsifted white flour

AT HOME:

Mix yeast and warm water in a large mixing bowl, and stir until dissolved. Mix in sugar, salt, butter, orange rind, and rye flour. Beat until thoroughly blended. Stir in enough white flour to form a stiff dough. Turn out onto a floured board and knead until smooth and elastic, about 12 minutes. Place in greased bowl; turn once to grease both sides. Cover, let rise in a warm place until double in bulk, about 1 hour. Punch dough down, divide into two parts, and roll each part into a 14" x 9" rectangle. Shape into loaves and place in two greased 9" x 5" loaf pans. Cover, let rise in a warm place until double in bulk, about 1 hour. Bake in a 375°F. oven 40 minutes, or until done. The loaves should sound hollow when thumped. Cool, wrap in plastic, and store in freezer.

SEVEN-GRAIN BREAD

>   2 packages active dry yeast
>   3 cups warm water
>   ½ cup honey
>   5–6 cups whole wheat flour
>   ¼ cup oil
>   2 teaspoons salt
>   ½ cup cornmeal
>   ½ cup oatmeal, uncooked
>   ¼ cup rye flour
>   ¼ cup buckwheat flour
>   ¼ cup soy flour
>   ¼ cup cracked millet

AT HOME:

Soften yeast in warm water until bubbly, about 10 minutes. Stir in honey. Add 4 cups whole wheat flour and beat vigorously. Let stand in a warm place 45 minutes. Add oil, salt, cornmeal, oatmeal, rye, buckwheat and soy flours, and cracked millet, beating each time until well mixed. Add enough whole wheat flour to form a firm dough, about 1½ cups. Turn out on an oiled surface and knead until smooth and elastic, 15 to 20 minutes. Put dough in greased bowl, covered, until it doubles, about 1 hour. Punch dough down, shape into two loaves, and put into two greased 9″ x 5″ loaf pans. Let rise until doubled, about 1 hour. Bake in a 350°F. oven until done, 50 minutes or 1 hour. Bread should sound hollow when thumped. Cool, wrap in plastic, and store in freezer.

ON THE TRAIL:

Slice and spread with peanut butter, cheese, or other sandwich spreads.

WHEAT GERM YOGHURT BREAD

    8–9 cups flour
    ¾ cup powdered milk
    5 teaspoons salt
    1 package active dry yeast
    2¾ cups water
    1 cup yoghurt
    ¼ cup honey
    2 tablespoons butter
    1 cup wheat germ
    1 egg, beaten

AT HOME:

Mix 3½ cups flour, milk, egg, salt, and yeast in a large mixing bowl. Combine water, yoghurt, honey, and butter and heat over low heat until warm. Add gradually to dry ingredients and beat well for 2 minutes. Add 1 cup flour, beat again for 2 minutes. Stir in wheat germ and enough flour to form a stiff dough. Turn out on a floured board and knead until smooth and elastic, about 10 minutes. Place in a greased bowl, turn over to grease both sides.

Cover and let rise in a warm place until doubled in bulk. Punch down dough, divide in half. Divide each half in 3 parts, and shape each part into a 16″ rope. Braid 3 ropes together, pinching ends to seal. Repeat with second half and place loaves on a greased baking tin. Cover and let rise in a warm place until doubled in bulk, about 1 hour. Bake in a 350°F. oven 40 minutes, or until done. Cool, wrap, and freeze.

IN CAMP:
Slice and toast, spread with butter. Or slice for sandwiches for lunch.

APRICOT NUT BREAD

> 2 cups whole wheat flour
> 4 teaspoons baking powder
> ½ teaspoon baking soda
> ½ teaspoon salt
> ½ cup sugar
> 1 egg, beaten
> 1 cup sour cream
> ¼ cup milk
> 2 tablespoons butter
> 1 tablespoon grated orange rind
> 1 cup bran
> ½ cup walnuts, chopped
> 1 cup dried apricots, cooked and minced

AT HOME:
Sift together dry ingredients. Cream sugar and butter, beat in egg, sour cream, and milk. Stir in bran, walnuts, orange rind, and apricots, and mix with flour. Pour batter into a greased 9″ x 5″ loaf pan and let stand 10 minutes. Bake in a 350°F. oven for 1 hour, or until it tests done when a toothpick is inserted in center and comes out clean. Cool, wrap in plastic, and freeze.

ON THE TRAIL:
Slice for lunch, snack, or dessert with cheese.

CARROT FRUIT BREAD

      2 cups flour
    ½ teaspoon salt
      1 teaspoon baking soda
      2 teaspoons baking powder
      4 eggs
      8 tablespoons (½ cup) oil
      1 cup sugar *or* ⅔ cup honey
      1 cup buttermilk
      1 teaspoon cinnamon
      1 teaspoon vanilla
      2 cups grated carrots
      1 cup shredded coconut
      1 cup chopped dates
      1 cup raisins
      1 cup walnuts, chopped

AT HOME:
Sift together dry ingredients. Beat eggs, add oil, sugar or honey, and buttermilk. Fold in sifted dry ingredients and mix well. Gradually add carrots, fruit, and nuts until batter is mixed thoroughly. Pour into two 9″ x 5″ loaf pans and bake in a 350°F. oven for 50 minutes, or until a toothpick thrust into the center comes out clean. Cool, package in plastic wrap, and freeze.

ON THE TRAIL:
Slice for lunch, snacks, or desserts.

SPICY FIG LOAF

      3 cups flour, sifted
      4 teaspoons baking powder
      1 teaspoon baking soda
      1 teaspoon salt
      1 teaspoon cinnamon
    ¾ teaspoon ginger
    ¾ cup sugar *or* ½ cup honey
    1½ cups quick oatmeal
      2 cups buttermilk
    ⅓ cup vegetable oil
    ½ cup pecans, chopped
    ¾ cup dried figs, chopped

AT HOME:
Sift together dry ingredients. Add oatmeal, nuts and figs. Mix buttermilk, honey (if used), and oil into dry mixture. Pour into greased 9″ x 5″ loaf pan. Bake in a 350°F. oven about 1 hour. Cool, remove from pan, and cool on rack. Wrap in plastic or foil and freeze.

ON THE TRAIL:
A nourishing snack or lunch, or dessert.

VARIATION:
If buttermilk is not available, add 2 tablespoons lemon juice to 2 cups milk.

Dodie Sway
Western Research Kitchens
Los Angeles, California

GRANOLA BREAD

   1 cup whole wheat flour
¾ cup bran
   1 teaspoon baking powder
   1 teaspoon baking soda
¼ teaspoon salt
½ cup (1 stick) margarine, softened
¼ cup molasses
½ cup honey
   1 egg
   1 cup plain yoghurt
   1 cup granola
¼ cup raisins

AT HOME:
Sift together flour and other dry ingredients. Beat together margarine, molasses, honey, and egg. Add flour alternately with yoghurt, blending well. Mix in granola and raisins, and pour into a 9″ x 5″ greased loaf pan. Bake for 1 hour in a 350°F. oven until done. Cool, slice, and wrap each slice in plastic. Store in refrigerator or freezer.

ON THE TRAIL:
Take along slices for any meal, or for snacks.

> *Candie Leunig*
> *Frostburg, Maryland*

GREG'S EVERLASTING BREAD

4½ cups whole wheat flour
3 teaspoons baking soda
½ cup whole powdered milk
½ teaspoon allspice, ground
½ teaspoon cloves, ground
1 teaspoon cinnamon
1 teaspoon salt
1 cup brown sugar
1 cup granulated sugar
1 cup vegetable shortening
2 tablespoons vinegar
2 cups water
1 cup raisins
1 cup nuts, chopped
1 cup dates, diced

AT HOME:
Sift dry ingredients. Cream sugar and shortening. Add sifted dry ingredients alternately with liquid until well blended. Add fruit and nuts. Pour batter into two greased 9″ x 5″ loaf pans and bake in a 325°F. oven 1 hour, or until the tops spring back when pressed. Cool, slice, and wrap each portion in plastic. Refrigerate or freeze.

ON THE TRAIL:
A nutritious meal that keeps well.

> *Greg Koebel*
> *Upper Montclair, New Jersey*

HONEY QUICK BREAD

2½ cups whole wheat flour
  1 teaspoon baking soda
  1 teaspoon cinnamon
  ¼ teaspoon nutmeg
  ½ teaspoon salt
  ¾ cup honey
  1 cup brown sugar
  1 cup chopped nuts and seeds—any kind
  ½ cup chopped dried fruit and/or raisins
  1 cup boiling water

AT HOME:
Sift dry ingredients together. Mix in honey and sugar, nuts and seeds, and fruits. Add boiling water and stir well. Pour into a greased and floured 9″ x 5″ loaf pan and fill two-thirds full. Bake in a 350°F. oven for 1½ hours. Cool, wrap in foil or plastic, and store in refrigerator.

ON THE TRAIL:
Slice for lunch or dinner. Good with Cheddar cheese.

Mary Belyea
Richmond Hill, Ontario

OATMEAL RAISIN BREAD

  1 cup oatmeal
  1 cup buttermilk
  ½ cup brown sugar
  1 egg, beaten
  1 cup whole wheat flour
  1 teaspoon baking powder
  1 teaspoon salt
  ½ teaspoon baking soda
  6 tablespoons (¾ stick) butter, melted
  ½ cup golden raisins

AT HOME:

Soak oatmeal in buttermilk 1 hour. Add sugar and well-beaten egg. Sift dry ingredients and mix with oatmeal, melted butter, and raisins. Pour batter into a greased 9″ x 5″ loaf pan. Bake in a 400°F. oven 40 minutes, or until a toothpick thrust into center comes out clean. Cool, wrap in plastic, and freeze.

ON THE TRAIL:

Eat buttered for breakfast, or with cheese for lunch.

ORANGE FIG BREAD

      2½ cups flour
        3 teaspoons baking powder
       ¾ teaspoon salt
      2½ cups figs, chopped finely
        2 tablespoons grated orange rind
        2 tablespoons orange juice concentrate
        1 cup boiling water
        2 tablespoons butter
      ⅔ cups honey
        1 egg, beaten
       ½ cup nuts, chopped

AT HOME:

Sift together dry ingredients. Mix figs, orange rind, orange juice concentrate with boiling water. Mix butter, honey, and beaten egg, then combine all ingredients. Mix in flour and fruit mixture alternately. Pour into two greased 9″ x 5″ loaf pans and bake in a 350°F. oven for 50 minutes, or until a toothpick thrust into the center of the loaves comes out clean. Cool, wrap in plastic, and freeze.

ON THE TRAIL:

Spread with cream cheese for breakfast or lunch.

PEACH NUT BREAD

  1¾ cups whole wheat flour
   ¼ cup wheat germ
   2 teaspoons baking powder
   ½ teaspoon baking soda
   1 teaspoon salt
   ½ teaspoon cinnamon
   ½ teaspoon cloves, ground
   2 tablespoons butter
   ⅔ cup brown sugar
   2 eggs, beaten
   2 cups dried peaches, diced
   ½ cup nuts, chopped

AT HOME:

Sift together dry ingredients. Mix butter, sugar, and beaten egg. Combine with dry ingredients and beat until well mixed. The batter will be stiff. Soak, drain, and chop peaches, and fold into batter with nuts. Pour into a greased 9″ x 5″ loaf pan and bake in a 350°F. oven 1 hour, or until a toothpick thrust into the center comes out clean. Cool on rack, wrap in plastic, and store in freezer.

ON THE TRAIL:

Eat for breakfast, snacks, lunch, or dinner.

PERSIMMON BREAD

  2½ cups flour
   1 teaspoon baking soda
   ½ teaspoon salt
   3 teaspoons baking powder
   ½ teaspoon cinnamon
   ½ teaspoon nutmeg
   2 eggs, beaten
   ⅔ cup milk
   ¼ cup (½ stick) butter, melted
   2 cups persimmon pulp
   1 teaspoon vanilla *or* lemon extract
   2 cups raisins *or* dates, chopped
   1 cup chopped nuts

AT HOME:
Sift together dry ingredients. Beat eggs, mix milk, melted butter, persimmon pulp, and extract. Mix with dry ingredients until thoroughly combined. Add fruit and nuts, beat well. Bake in two greased 9″ x 5″ loaf pans in a 350°F. oven for 1 hour, or until loaves test done when a toothpick is inserted and comes out clean. Cool, wrap in plastic, and freeze.

ON THE TRAIL:
Slice for breakfast, lunch, dinner, or snacks.

PUMPKIN BREAD

        3½ cups flour
         2 teaspoons baking soda
        1½ teaspoons salt
         1 teaspoon cinnamon
         1 teaspoon nutmeg
         4 eggs, beaten
        ½ cup sugar
         1 cup honey
         1 cup oil
         2 cups cooked pumpkin
        ½ cup pecans, chopped

AT HOME:
Sift together dry ingredients. Beat eggs, mix in sugar, honey, oil, and pumpkin. Mix with dry ingredients and beat well. Add nuts. Pour into two greased 9″ x 5″ loaf pans and bake in a 350°F. oven for 1 hour, or until loaves test done when a toothpick is inserted and comes out clean. Cool, wrap in plastic, and freeze.

ON THE TRAIL:
Toast for breakfast, or make sandwiches with cheese or dried meats.

WALNUT VEGETABLE BREAD

    1 cup white flour
    1 teaspoon baking powder
   ½ teaspoon baking soda
    1 teaspoon salt
    1 cup whole wheat flour, unsifted
   ½ cup sugar
   ½ teaspoon dill weed
    2 eggs, beaten
   ½ cup milk
   ⅓ cup vegetable oil
    1 cup carrots, grated
   ½ cup celery, minced
   ⅔ cup walnuts, chopped finely

AT HOME:

Sift together dry ingredients except whole wheat flour and dill weed. Beat eggs, add milk and oil, and combine with white flour mixture. Add whole wheat flour and dill weed. Add carrots, celery, and walnuts. Mix well with each addition. Pour batter into greased 9″ x 5″ loaf pan. Let stand 15 minutes. Bake in a 350°F. oven for 1 hour, or until loaf tests done when a toothpick is inserted. Cool, wrap in plastic, and freeze.

ON THE TRAIL:

Eat for lunch, buttered or with cheese.

ZUCCHINI BREAD

    3 cups sifted flour
    1 teaspoon salt
    1 teaspoon baking soda
    3 teaspoons cinnamon
   ¼ teaspoon baking powder
    1 cup sugar
    1 cup brown sugar
    1 cup salad oil
    3 eggs
    2 cups grated zucchini
    3 teaspoons vanilla
   ½ cup nuts, chopped

AT HOME:

Mix together dry ingredients. In a separate bowl, mix together sugars, oil, and eggs. Beat well. Add zucchini and vanilla. Mix with flour, and add nuts. Pour into two greased, lightly floured 9″ x 5″ loaf pans. Bake in a 325°F. oven for 1 hour, or until a toothpick inserted in the center comes out clean. Cool, wrap in plastic, and freeze.

VARIATION:

Zucchini bread may be baked in coffee cans and carried along in the cans. If baked in coffee cans, bake 15 minutes longer.

Eric H. Natvig
Sioux Falls, South Dakota

APPLESAUCE CAKE

    1½ cups whole wheat flour
     1 teaspoon baking soda
     1 teaspoon allspice
     2 teaspoons ginger
    ½ cup oil
     1 cup brown sugar *or* ⅔ cup honey
     1 cup applesauce, unsweetened
    ½ cup dates, chopped

AT HOME:

Mix together dry ingredients. Mix oil, sugar or honey, applesauce, and dates, and mix with flour. Pour into greased 9″ x 5″ loaf pan. Bake in a 375°F. oven for 30 or 35 minutes. Cool, wrap in plastic, and freeze.

IN CAMP:

Eat for lunch, or for dessert with dinner.

BANANA SPICE CAKE

     2 cups flour
     1 teaspoon baking powder
     1 teaspoon salt
     1 teaspoon cinnamon
     1 teaspoon nutmeg
     2 eggs, beaten
     ½ cup honey
     ½ cup oil
     1 cup banana, mashed
     1 cup raisins
     ½ cup sunflower seeds or toasted nuts, chopped

AT HOME:
Sift together dry ingredients. Beat eggs, mix in honey, oil, and banana until smooth. Add flour, raisins, and seeds or nuts, and beat until well blended. Pour into a greased 9″ x 5″ loaf pan and bake in a 350°F. oven for 1 hour. Cool, wrap in foil or plastic, and freeze.

IN CAMP:
Serve for dessert with berries and cream.

BUTTER POUND CAKE

     1 lb. (4 sticks) butter
     2 cups sugar
     6 eggs, separated
     2 tablespoons grated lemon rind
     4 cups flour
     1 lb. raisins
     ¼ cup flour
     ½ cup walnut halves

AT HOME:
Cream together butter and sugar and beat 15 minutes. Beat egg yolks and add to mixture with lemon rind. Fold in stiffly beaten

egg whites. Add flour gradually, and mix well. Dredge raisins in ¼ cup flour and fold into mixture, stirring in thoroughly. Line two 9" x 5" loaf pans with waxed paper well greased with butter. Pour batter into tins and top with walnut halves. Bake in a 325°F. oven for about 1½ hours. Cool for 1 hour in pans. Remove from pans, wrap in foil, and freeze.

IN CAMP:
Eat buttered for lunch, or topped with berries and cream for dessert.

BAKING INSTRUCTIONS FOR FRUITCAKES

1. Be sure the oven is *not* too hot. Fruit and sugar burn easily.
2. A pan of water on the lower oven rack will create steam and retard burning.
3. A piece of aluminum foil placed lightly across tops of fruitcake pans will prevent their browning too fast.

Pan Sizes and Approximate Baking Times
(Slow oven, 300°–325°F.)

1. An 8½" x 4½" x 2¾" loaf pan holds 4 cups batter, takes about 2 hours to bake.
2. A 4½" x 3" x 2½" loaf pan holds 1¾–2 cups batter, takes 1½ hours to bake.
3. A 3-quart tube pan or mold holds about 2½ quarts batter, takes 2½ to 3 hours to bake.
4. A 7½" ring mold holds 3 cups batter, takes 1¾ hours to bake.
5. Muffin tins or cupcake pans, 1¾" x ¾" will each hold 1–2 tablespoons batter, take 20 minutes to bake.

BOILED FRUITCAKE

½ cup sugar *or* honey
½ cup molasses
½ cup oil
1 cup raisins
1 tablespoon cinnamon
½ teaspoon nutmeg
½ teaspoon cloves
1 cup water
2 cups flour
3 tablespoons wheat germ
1 teaspoon baking soda
1 teaspoon salt
1 egg, beaten
½ cup nuts, chopped

AT HOME:
Add sugar or honey, molasses, oil, raisins and spices to water and simmer for 20 minutes. Sift together dry ingredients. When cooked mixture has cooled, stir in beaten egg and flour mixture, and nuts. Mix thoroughly. Pour into greased 9″ x 5″ loaf pan and bake in a 350°F. oven for 45 minutes, or until a toothpick inserted in center comes out clean. Cool, wrap in foil, and store in a cool place.

ON THE TRAIL:
Eat slices for lunch, snacks, or dessert.

FRUITCAKE I

    ¾ cup sugar
    ½ cup (1 stick) butter *or* margarine
    1 egg, beaten
    ¼ cup strong coffee
    1 cup applesauce
    2½ cups flour
    1 teaspoon baking soda
    1 teaspoon salt
    ¼ teaspoon cinnamon
    ½ teaspoon cloves
    ¼ teaspoon allspice
    1 cup candied fruits, chopped
    ½ cup dates, chopped
    ½ cup raisins
    1 cup figs, chopped
    1 cup nuts, chopped

AT HOME:
Cream sugar and butter. Beat egg and add to mixture. Stir in coffee and applesauce. Mix together dry ingredients and beat into mixture. Fold in fruit and nuts 1 cup at a time. Pour batter into two greased 9″ x 5″ loaf pans lined with waxed paper. Bake in a 325°F. oven for 1¼ hours. Cool, wrap in foil, and store in a cool place.

IN CAMP:
Eat for lunch, snacks, or as dinner dessert.

FRUITCAKE II

       2 cups flour
       2 teaspoons baking powder
    ½ teaspoon salt
       3 cups dates, pitted and chopped
       1 lb. candied pineapple, chopped
       1 lb. candied cherries, red and green
       1 lb. almonds, walnuts, and/or Brazil nuts, chopped
       4 eggs, beaten
       1 cup sugar *or* honey
       1 teaspoon vanilla
       1 tablespoon rum

AT HOME:
Sift together dry ingredients and mix with fruits and nuts. Beat eggs and add sugar or honey and flavoring, mixing thoroughly. Pour into dry ingredients and mix thoroughly. Line loaf pans with greased waxed paper and fill with batter three-quarters full. Place a pan of water on lower shelf in oven to keep cakes moist. Bake in a 250°F. oven. Time depends on size of pans (p. 149). When baked, cool on racks. Wrap in cloths moistened in brandy, rum, or sherry, and store in a cool place.

ON THE TRAIL:
Eat slices for snacks, or for dessert.

MINCEMEAT CAKE

    2½ cups flour
       1 teaspoon baking soda
       2 eggs, beaten
    2½ cups mincemeat
       1 can (14 oz.) condensed milk
       1 cup walnuts and pecans, chopped
    ½ cup candied fruit, chopped
    ½ candied citrus rind, chopped
    ½ cup candied ginger, minced
    ½ cup figs and dates, chopped

AT HOME:
Sift together dry ingredients. Beat eggs, add mincemeat, milk, fruits, and nuts. Fold in flour and blend well. Pour batter into two 9" x 5" greased loaf pans lined with waxed paper. Bake in a 300°F. oven for 1 hour, or until toothpick inserted in center comes out clean. Cool on rack, remove waxed paper. Wrap in foil and store in a cool place.

ON THE TRAIL:
Eat for lunch, snacks, or dessert.

GINGERBREAD

        2 cups flour
        2 teaspoons ginger
      ¾ teaspoon baking soda
      ¾ teaspoon salt
      ¼ cup oil
      ½ cup brown sugar
        1 egg
      ½ cup molasses
      ½ cup milk

AT HOME:
Sift together dry ingredients. Mix oil and sugar, add egg and beat well. Add molasses and milk and mix. Add flour gradually until batter is smooth. Pour into a greased 9" square baking pan and bake in a 350°F. oven until done, about 30 minutes. Cool, cut into squares, and wrap each in plastic. Store in freezer.

IN CAMP:
Gingerbread topped with applesauce is good for breakfast, lunch, or dinner.

Cookies, Candies, Trail Snacks, & Puddings

BACKPACKING BARS

½ cup (1 stick) butter *or* margarine
½ cup brown sugar
¾ cup flour
½ cup oatmeal
¼ cup wheat germ, toasted
1 tablespoon grated orange rind
2 eggs, beaten
¼ cup brown sugar
½ cup shredded coconut
4½ oz. almonds, slivered

AT HOME:
Cream together butter and sugar until fluffy. Mix in dry ingredients until well blended. Press mixture into a greased 8" square baking pan. Beat eggs with remaining brown sugar. Stir in coconut and almonds. Pour evenly over mixture in pan. Bake in a 350°F. oven for 25 minutes, or until a toothpick inserted in center comes out clean. Cool, and cut into 12 bars. Wrap each in plastic and store in tins in a cool place.

ON THE TRAIL:
Take along bars for breakfast, lunch or snacks.

Kaye Manchester
Crystal Lake, Illinois

BACKPACK SNACK BARS

      1 can (6 oz.) frozen orange juice concentrate, thawed
    ½ cup quick oats
    ½ cup dried apricots, sliced
    ½ cup prunes, pitted and diced
    ½ cup raisins
    ¼ cup walnuts, chopped
    ¼ cup pecans, roasted and chopped
    ¼ cup dates, diced
    ¼ cup wheat germ
      1 tablespoon sesame seeds
    ½ cup vegetable shortening
    ½ cup raw sugar
    ½ cup molasses
      1 large egg, beaten
      2 cups all-purpose flour
    ¼ teaspoon baking soda
      1 teaspoon ginger
      1 teaspoon cinnamon

AT HOME:
Mix together thawed fruit juice, oats, fruit, nuts, and wheat germ. In another bowl, cream together shortening and sugar. Add molasses and beaten egg. Sift in dry ingredients and stir. Add fruit and nut mixture slowly. Blend well. Pour into greased 9″ x 13″ baking pan and bake in a 325°F. oven for 35 minutes. Cool, cut into 1″ x 3″ bars. Wrap each in plastic or foil and store in refrigerator or freezer. Makes about 39 bars.

ON THE TRAIL:
Take along two bars per person per day for trail snacks.

Carron Sundberg
Delta, British Columbia

BANANA OAT ENERGY BARS

   ¾ cup butter *or* margarine
   1 cup brown sugar, packed
   1 egg
   ½ teaspoon salt
   1½ cups ripe bananas, mashed
        (4 or 5 medium-sized bananas)
   4 cups regular oatmeal
   1 cup raisins *or* chocolate chips
   ½ cup walnuts *or* pecans, chopped

AT HOME:
Cream butter and sugar until fluffy. Beat in egg, salt, and bananas. Mix in remaining ingredients until well blended. Pour into a greased 9″ x 12″ pan. Bake in a 350°F. oven for 1 hour, or until toothpick inserted in center comes out clean. Cool, cut into 2″ bars. Wrap each in plastic and store in refrigerator.

ON THE TRAIL:
Bars may be eaten for breakfast, lunch or snacks.

Jacqueline Jones
San Diego, California

MINCEMEAT BARS

   1¼ cups flour, sifted
    ¾ cup brown sugar
    1 cup quick oatmeal, uncooked
    ½ teaspoon salt
    ½ cup margarine (1 stick)
    1 box (9 oz.) condensed mincemeat, cooked
   2–3 tablespoons milk

AT HOME:
Mix dry ingredients and cut in margarine until crumbly. Spread half of mixture on bottom of 8″ square baking pan. Cover with

mincemeat. Then cover mincemeat with rest of dry mixture. Pat down smoothly and sprinkle with milk. Bake in a 400°F. oven for 30 minutes. Cool, cut into 2″ bars. Wrap each in plastic and store in refrigerator. Makes 16 bars.

VARIATION:
Stir in 2 tablespoons brandy after mincemeat is cooked. Mix mincemeat with dry mixture and bake.

Gordon J. Koncelik
Hollywood, Florida

MOUNTAIN BARS

    1 package (6 oz.) butterscotch chips
    ¼ cup honey
    ¼ cup raisins
    ¼ cup coconut, flaked
    ¼ cup walnuts, chopped
    ½ cup wheat germ
    ½ cup oatmeal

AT HOME:
Melt butterscotch chips over low heat in saucepan. Stir in honey until well blended. Add other ingredients and stir until well mixed. Remove from heat and pour into greased baking pan. Cool, cut into 2″ squares, and wrap each square tightly in plastic. Store in refrigerator.

ON THE TRAIL:
Take along bars for a trail snack.

Stephen C. Plog
Los Angeles, California

TRAIL MUNCHIES

        1 large egg
        1 teaspoon vanilla
        ½ cup dark brown sugar, packed
        ½ cup maple syrup
        1 cup (2 sticks) butter
        1 cup all-purpose flour
        ⅔ cup rolled oats
        3 cups granola with raisins and dates
        1 can (14 oz.) condensed milk

AT HOME:
Mix egg, vanilla, sugar, syrup, and butter, and cream until fluffy. Stir in remaining ingredients gradually until thoroughly mixed. Spread on an ungreased 11" x 17" baking sheet. Bake in a 350°F. oven for 30 minutes. Cool, cut into 2" x 4" bars. Makes 20 bars. Wrap each in plastic and store in refrigerator.

ON THE TRAIL:
Take along bars for breakfast, lunch, or snacks.

Carol Chab and Ken Karsmizki
Bloomington, Indiana

CAROB (*St. John's Bread*)

The fruit of the carob tree (a member of the legume family) resembles an overgrown lima-bean pod. Carob is particularly useful for people who are allergic to chocolate, and many health foods are made with it. Carob powder may be substituted evenly for cocoa; 3 tablespoons of powder plus 1 tablespoon of fat may be substituted for 1 ounce of baking chocolate. Carob is also available in chips that resemble chocolate chips.

CAROB CHIP COOKIES

   1¼ cups whole wheat flour
    1 teaspoon baking powder
   ½ teaspoon salt
   ½ teaspoon allspice
    4 tablespoons wheat germ
   ½ cup (1 stick) butter
   ½ cup honey
    1 egg, beaten
    1 teaspoon vanilla
    1 cup carob chips
    1 cup walnuts and pecans, chopped

AT HOME:
Sift together dry ingredients. Add wheat germ. Cream butter and honey and combine with beaten egg and vanilla. Mix with dry ingredients, add carob chips and nuts. Mix well. Drop by teaspoonfuls on greased baking sheet. Bake in a 400°F. oven for 15 minutes. Cool, store in closed tin in a cool place. Makes 3–4 dozen cookies.

ON THE TRAIL:
Take along a plastic bag of cookies for snacks.

CAROB NUT COOKIES

   1⅛ cups whole wheat flour
    3 tablespoons carob powder
   ½ teaspoon baking powder
   ¼ teaspoon baking soda
   ½ teaspoon salt
   ½ cup (1 stick) butter
   ¾ cup brown sugar
    1 egg, beaten
   1½ teaspoons vanilla
   ½ cup chopped nuts and toasted sunflower seeds
   ½ cup raisins *or* dates, chopped finely

AT HOME:
Sift together dry ingredients. Cream butter and sugar, add egg and vanilla. Mix with dry ingredients. Add nuts and fruit and mix well. Drop by teaspoonfuls on greased baking sheet. Bake in 400°F. oven for 15 minutes. Makes about 3 dozen cookies. Cool, store in closed tin in a cool place.

VARIATION:
Substitute shredded coconut for raisins and dates.

CANNONBALLS (HOCKEY PUCKS)

    1 cup whole wheat flour
    ½ teaspoon soda
    ¼ teaspoon salt
    ¾ cup brown sugar
    ½ cup shortening, softened
    1 large egg, beaten
    1 teaspoon vanilla
    ¼ cup milk
    ¼ cup powdered milk
    2 cups granola

AT HOME:
Mix together dry ingredients. Cream sugar and shortening, and mix in egg, milk, and vanilla. Stir in powdered milk and granola. The mixture will be stiff. Drop by teaspoonfuls on greased baking sheet. If left round, they are *cannonballs;* if flattened, *hockey pucks.* Bake 10 minutes in a 350°F. oven. Mixture may also be rolled into a 1" thick roll, then frozen until needed. Cut roll into 1" thick slices and bake on a greased baking sheet. Makes 18 to 24. Cool, store in closed tin in a cool place.

ON THE TRAIL:
Take along several in a plastic bag for snacks.

Susan H. Hirsch
Los Angeles, California

GINGERSNAPS

   3 cups sifted flour
1½ teaspoons baking soda
  ½ teaspoon salt
  3 teaspoons ginger
  ½ cup vegetable oil
  1 cup blackstrap molasses

AT HOME:
Sift together dry ingredients. Mix oil and molasses together and stir into dry ingredients. Stir well until dough is smooth. Chill and roll out on floured board to ¼″ thickness. Cut with a biscuit cutter or a small juice can. Bake on greased baking sheets in a 375°F. oven for 10 minutes. Cool, store in closed tin in a cool place. Makes 4–5 dozen gingersnaps.

ON THE TRAIL:
Take along gingersnaps in plastic bag for lunch, snacks, or dessert with fruit or puddings.

GINGER-CURRANT COOKIES

2½ cups flour
 2 teaspoons baking soda
 ½ teaspoon salt
 3 teaspoons ginger
 ¼ cup (½ stick) butter
 ½ cup brown sugar
 ½ cup molasses
 2 eggs, beaten
 1 cup currants

AT HOME:
Sift together dry ingredients. Cream butter with sugar and molasses. Add eggs. Mix with dry ingredients. Add currants, mix well. Drop by teaspoonfuls on a greased baking sheet. Bake in a 400°F. oven for 10 minutes. Cool, store in a closed tin in a cool place. Makes about 4 dozen cookies.

ON THE TRAIL:
Take along cookies for snacks or lunch.

PEANUT COOKIES

  1½ cups white flour
  ½ teaspoon cream of tartar
  ½ teaspoon baking soda
  ½ teaspoon cloves
  ½ teaspoon allspice
  ½ cup (1 stick) butter
  1 cup brown sugar
  1 egg, beaten
  ½ cup peanuts, roasted and chopped finely

AT HOME:
Sift together dry ingredients. Cream butter and sugar and add beaten egg. Mix with dry ingredients. Add peanuts and mix in well. Form dough in a roll, about 1″ in diameter. Wrap in waxed paper, and chill. Slice cookies ¼″ thick and bake on a greased baking sheet in a 425°F. oven for 10 minutes. Cool, store in a tin in a cool place.

ON THE TRAIL:
Take along a plastic bag for snacks with fruit.

VARIATION:
Use other nuts or seeds, or a mixture of both. Add 2 tablespoons carob powder or cocoa, for a chocolate-flavored cookie.

PUMPKIN COOKIES

1½ cups flour
1 teaspoon baking powder
1 teaspoon cinnamon
½ teaspoon ginger
¼ teaspoon cloves
½ teaspoon salt
⅓ cup butter
⅔ cup honey
1 cup cooked pumpkin
1 egg, beaten
1½ cups granola with nuts and raisins

AT HOME:
Sift together dry ingredients. Cream butter and honey, mix in pumpkin and beaten egg. Mix with dry ingredients, stirring until well mixed. Mix in granola. Drop by teaspoonfuls on a greased baking sheet. Bake in a 375°F. oven 15 minutes. Cool, store in a closed tin in a cool place. Makes 4–5 dozen cookies.

RAISIN SAFARI COOKIES

¾ cup sifted flour
1¾ cups quick oatmeal
¼ teaspoon baking soda
1 teaspoon salt
1 teaspoon cinnamon
1½ cups golden raisins
1½ cups boiling water
2 eggs, beaten
¼ cup peanut butter
1 cup (2 sticks) butter
1 cup brown sugar
1 teaspoon vanilla

AT HOME:
Mix together dry ingredients. Cover raisins with boiling water

and let stand 5 minutes. Drain well. Beat eggs and mix in peanut butter, butter, sugar, and vanilla. Mix with dry ingredients and raisins until thoroughly mixed. Drop by teaspoonfuls on greased baking sheet. Bake in a 375°F. oven 15 minutes. Cool, store in a closed tin in a cool place. Makes about 4 dozen cookies.

ON THE TRAIL:
Take along cookies for lunch with fruit.

APLETS

> 2½ cups applesauce
> 4 envelopes plain gelatin
> 4 cups sugar *or* 3 cups honey
> 1 teaspoon vanilla
> 1 cup nuts, chopped fine
> ¼ cup powdered sugar

AT HOME:
Mix 1 cup applesauce with gelatin. Add rest of applesauce to sugar or honey, and combine mixtures. Cook 15 minutes. Remove from heat and add vanilla and nuts. Mix well and pour into 9″ x 12″ baking pan and cool. Cut into squares and roll each in powdered sugar. Wrap in plastic and store in refrigerator. Makes about 48 squares.

ON THE TRAIL:
Take along for lunch or snack.

VARIATION:
Substitute apricot purée for the applesauce to make "cotlets."

CAROB CANDY

½ cup carob powder
¼ cup wheat germ
¼ cup soy flour
½ teaspoon salt
½ cup sunflower seeds
½ cup sesame seeds
½ cup honey
½ cup natural peanut butter
½ cup unsweetened grated coconut

AT HOME:
Mix dry ingredients together, then add honey and peanut butter. The mixture will be stiff and will require much kneading with wooden spoon or hands. Form into balls and roll each ball in coconut. Makes 40 to 50 balls about ¾ inch in diameter, or weighing about 1⅔ lbs. Store in a tin in a cool place.

ON THE TRAIL:
Tie half a dozen balls into a plastic bag for lunch or snacks.

Rosemary Griffith
Westfield, New Jersey

CAROB FUDGE

6 tablespoons carob powder
2 cups sugar
¼ teaspoon salt
⅔ cup milk
2 tablespoons butter
1 teaspoon vanilla

AT HOME:
Combine carob, sugar, salt, and milk. Cook over low heat until sugar is dissolved, stirring occasionally. Increase heat and bring to a boil. Cook until mixture reaches soft ball stage (225° to 230°F.).

Remove from heat, add butter and vanilla, and beat until mixture begins to thicken. Pour into an oiled 9″ square pan and let cool. Cut into squares. Makes 25. Wrap each in plastic and store in refrigerator.

ON THE TRAIL:
Take along several squares for lunch or snack.

CHOCOLATE BOMBERS

   ½ cup (1 stick) butter
 1½ oz. unsweetened chocolate
   2 eggs
   1 cup sugar
   1 teaspoon vanilla
   ¾ cup mincemeat
   ¾ cup flour
   ¼ teaspoon salt
   ½ cup chopped walnuts
   ½ cup chocolate chips

AT HOME:
Melt butter and chocolate. Beat eggs, adding sugar while beating. Stir in vanilla and mincemeat. Blend in flour, salt, nuts, and chocolate chips. Add chocolate mixture and mix well. Pour into lightly greased 9″ x 9″ pan and bake in a 350°F. oven about 30 minutes. Cool, cut into squares and wrap in plastic or foil. Store in freezer. Makes 12 to 18, depending on size of squares.

ON THE TRAIL:
Take along one per person for snacks.

Lauren S. Waite
Seattle, Washington

WHEAT GERM BROWNIES

4 squares unsweetened chocolate
¾ cup margarine
1¼ cup flour
2 teaspoons baking powder
1 teaspoon salt
1 cup wheat germ
¼ cup brown sugar, firmly packed
1 cup granulated sugar
3 eggs, well beaten
1 teaspoon vanilla
⅓ cup chocolate chips
⅓ cup chopped nuts

AT HOME:
Melt chocolate and margarine in saucepan in oven. (Melting is slower and more even than on stove top.) Sift together dry ingredients. Mix sugars and eggs and add to dry mixture. Add vanilla and stir in melted chocolate mixture. Fold in chocolate chips and nuts and spread mixture in a greased 9″ x 13″ x 2″ pan. Bake in a 350°F. oven for 30 to 35 minutes. Cool, cut in squares, and wrap each in waxed paper or plastic. Store in refrigerator.

ON THE TRAIL:
Good for lunch or snacks.

Carla J. Hoff
McKinleysville, California

FUDGE SCOTCH SQUARES

1½ cups graham cracker crumbs
1 can (14 oz.) sweetened condensed milk
1 cup semisweet chocolate chips
1 cup butterscotch chips
1 cup coarsely chopped walnuts

AT HOME:
Mix ingredients together well and press mixture into a well-

greased 9″ square pan. Bake in a 350°F. oven for 30 to 35 minutes. Cool for 45 minutes, cut into squares, and remove from pan. Wrap each in plastic or waxed paper and store in refrigerator.

ON THE TRAIL:
Take along for lunch or snack.

> *Jennifer Loomis*
> *Monterey, California*

MUNCHY CUBES

   2 8-oz. bars German's sweet chocolate
1¼ cups raisins
1¼ cups Spanish peanuts
1¼ cups Rice Krispies

AT HOME:
Melt the chocolate slowly in a double boiler. Add other ingredients slowly, stirring continuously, until everything is well coated with chocolate. Spoon mixture into plastic ice-cube trays and press into cubes gently. Freeze for 15 minutes. Makes approximately 30 cubes.

ON THE TRAIL:
Keep cool, for lunch or snack.

> *George W. Lilley, Jr.*
> *Athens, West Virginia*

COFFEE NUGGETS

½ cup (1 stick) butter
 3 tablespoons powdered sugar
 1 teaspoon vanilla
 1 tablespoon instant coffee
 1 cup flour, sifted
½ cup pecans, chopped fine

AT HOME:
Cream butter, sugar, vanilla and coffee until light and fluffy. Add flour and nuts, slowly, mixing well. Chill dough. Roll into 1" balls and bake on a greased baking tin in a 350°F. oven for 15 minutes. Cool, store in a covered tin in a cool place. Makes about 24.

ON THE TRAIL:
Take along for lunch or snack.

CANDIED CITRUS PEEL

    4 cups slivered citrus peels
    6 cups sugar
    6 cups water

AT HOME:
Scrape white pith from citrus peels and cut peels in strips 1/2" wide. Put in pot of boiling water and let soak 5 minutes, then drain. Put peels into a second pot of boiling water and boil 10 minutes. Drain again. Repeat third time, remove from water and drain.

Dissolve sugar in 6 cups water and boil 5 minutes. Add peels, lower heat, and let simmer 10 minutes. Remove peels, bring syrup to a boil and cook until it reaches 240°F. on a candy thermometer. Add peels and simmer over low heat until translucent, 20 to 40 minutes. Remove peels from syrup and spread on waxed paper to cool and dry. Store in covered tins. Use in fruitcakes, or as candy for the trail.

FRUIT BALLS

    1/2 cup *each:* dried peaches, pears, apricots,
                    prunes, papaya, crystallized ginger
    1/4 cup raisins *or* currants
    1/4 cup wheat germ
    1/4 cup powdered sugar

AT HOME:
Chop fruits fine. Mix with wheat germ and roll into 1″ or 2″ balls. Roll in powdered sugar and store in tins in a cool place.

ON THE TRAIL:
Package several balls in a plastic bag for lunch or snack.

VARIATION:
Melt 6 oz. semisweet chocolate. Lay balls on waxed paper and pour chocolate over each, turning to cover fruit thoroughly. Chill, wrap each in plastic, and store in refrigerator.

MEDITERRANEAN FRUIT BALLS

    2 cups dates, pitted
    2 cups prunes, pitted
    2 cups raisins
    1 cup figs
    1 lemon, grated and squeezed
    1 cup finely chopped nuts

AT HOME:
Grind all fruits through medium blade of food grinder. Add grated lemon peel and juice. Shape into small balls 1″ to 1½″ in diameter and roll balls in nuts. Yields about 200 balls. Mixture may be frozen, then thawed and formed into balls when needed.

ON THE TRAIL:
Take along balls in plastic bags for lunch or snacks.

Mary L. Kibling
Concord, New Hampshire

PEMMICAN FRUIT BARS

    1 lb. dried dates
    4 oz. dried apricots
    4 oz. prunes, pitted
    4 oz. candied pineapple
    4 oz. golden raisins
    4 tablespoons coconut, grated
    1 cup mixed nuts, chopped
    ¼ cup powdered sugar

AT HOME:
Chop fruit and mix all ingredients together. Grind mixture with coarsest blade of food grinder. Dust a baking pan with powdered sugar. Mash fruit mixture into a flat slab on baking pan and cut into bars. Cover each bar with more powdered sugar. Store on a cool shelf, cover, and let dry for two weeks. Makes 30 bars. Wrap each in plastic foil and store in tins. Will keep for many months.

ON THE TRAIL:
Take bars along for snacks or desserts.

VARIATION:
Substitute candied fruits or grapefruit rind for candied pineapple.

Wilson E. Yetter
Ithaca, New York

SEED SQUARES

    2 cups sesame seeds
    1 cup sunflower seeds
    ¼ cup carob powder
    ½ cup honey
    ½ cup hot water
    ¼ teaspoon salt
    1 teaspoon vanilla

AT HOME:
Grind seeds and combine with other ingredients. Spread mixture on greased baking tin to a ½" thickness. Dry in a 200°F. oven with door slightly ajar for 1 hour or longer, until mixture is firm. Cut in 2" squares, wrap in plastic, and store in refrigerator.

ON THE TRAIL:
Take along several squares for lunch or snack.

VARIATION:
Add 2 tablespoons chia seeds, or grind 1 tablespoon fenugreek seeds in mixture.

BACKPACKER'S DELIGHT

  1 lb. old-fashioned (unhomogenized) peanut butter
  1 cup honey
  ¼ cup powdered yeast
  ¼ cup soy lecithin
  ¼ cup Tiger's Milk
  ¼ cup sesame seeds
  ¼ cup chia seeds
  ¼ cup wheat germ
  ½ cup raisins *or* currants
  1 cup mixed nuts, crushed
  1 teaspoon sea salt *or* crushed kelp

AT HOME:
Mix together all ingredients and form into 1" or 1½" balls. Roll in wheat germ or nuts, and store in a tin in a cool place.

ON THE TRAIL:
Eat for lunch with fruit.

VARIATION:
Substitute other nut butters and add sunflower seed oil. Roll balls in grated coconut.

P. Lee
Arlington, Virginia

CRUNCH BALLS

    2 cups crunchy peanut butter
    1 cup honey
    3 cups oatmeal
    ¼ teaspoon vanilla
    ¼ teaspoon salt
    ½ cup crushed nuts

AT HOME:
Heat peanut butter and honey until mixture is slightly liquid. Stir in oatmeal, vanilla, salt, and nuts. When cool, form into about 15 balls. Wrap each in plastic and store in refrigerator.

ON THE TRAIL:
Take along for lunch with fruit.

Casey Christensen
Powell, Wyoming

GRUNCH

    1 cup crunchy peanut butter
    ½ cup honey
    ½ cup honey graham crackers, crushed
    ¼ cup powdered milk
    3 teaspoons cinnamon
    1 teaspoon cloves

AT HOME:
Mix all ingredients thoroughly. Pack in a screw-top plastic container and keep cool. Makes 2 cups of spread.

ON THE TRAIL:
Spread mixture on crackers or bread for lunch, or eat with a spoon as a snack.

Rick Ford
Seattle, Washington

PEANUT BUTTER BALLS

 1 cup crunchy peanut butter
 ½ cup powdered milk
 1 cup raisins *or* currants
 ¼ cup wheat germ
 ¼ cup honey
 ¼ cup sesame seeds

AT HOME:
Mix together all ingredients except sesame seeds until well blended. Roll into balls 1″ to 1½″ in diameter, and roll each ball in sesame seeds until well covered. Package in plastic bags and store in refrigerator.

ON THE TRAIL:
Take along a bag of several balls for lunch.

PEANUT BUTTER SQUARES

 ½ cup sugar
 ½ cup corn syrup
 ¾ cup peanut butter
 ⅛ teaspoon salt
 1 cup Rice Krispies
 2 cups cornflakes
 1 teaspoon vanilla

AT HOME:
Melt sugar and syrup in a pan. Add peanut butter, salt, cereals, and vanilla and mix well. Spread in a 9″ x 15″ greased baking pan and cool. When cold, cut into 2″ squares. Makes about 30. Wrap in plastic and store in refrigerator.

ON THE TRAIL:
Take along squares for snacks or lunch.

PEANUT BUTTER FUDGE

    2 cups sugar
    2 tablespoons corn syrup
    ¼ teaspoon salt
    ⅔ cup milk
    ½ cup peanut butter
    1 teaspoon vanilla

AT HOME:
Combine sugar, syrup, salt and milk and cook over low heat until sugar is dissolved, stirring occasionally. Increase heat and bring to a boil. Cook until mixture reaches soft ball stage (225° to 230°F.). Remove from heat, stir in peanut butter and vanilla. Beat until mixture begins to thicken, and pour into a greased 9″ square pan. Cool, cut into squares. Makes about 25. Wrap each in plastic and refrigerate.

ON THE TRAIL:
One or two squares are good for a snack.

PEANUT POLKA DOTTIES

    1½ cups quick rolled oats
     1 can (14 oz.) sweetened condensed milk
    ½ teaspoon salt
     1 teaspoon vanilla
    ½ cup chunky peanut butter
    12 oz. semisweet chocolate chips

AT HOME:
Mix together oats, milk, salt, and vanilla. Stir in peanut butter and chocolate chips. Press mixture into a 8″ greased square baking pan. Bake in a 350°F. oven for 30 minutes. Cool, cut in squares, and wrap in plastic or waxed paper. Store in refrigerator.

ON THE TRAIL:
Take along squares for between-meal snacks.

B. C. Brunges
San Jose, California

HIKER'S DELIGHT

    3 cups golden raisins
    2 cups dried apricots, chopped
    2 cups cashews, walnuts, *or* other nuts
    2 cups sunflower seeds
    2 cups chocolate chips

AT HOME:
Mix all ingredients together. Store in plastic bags in refrigerator.

ON TRAIL:
Give each hiker a bag of the mix for trail snacks.

Roberts DeWitt
Haverhill, Massachusetts

FRUIT AND SEED TRAIL MIX

1½ cups rolled oatmeal
 ½ cup shredded coconut
 ½ cup sesame seeds
 ½ cup sunflower seeds
  4 tablespoons chia seeds
 ¼ lb. currants *or* raisins
 ¼ lb. dried pineapple, chopped
  2 oz. crystallized ginger, chopped fine
  2 tablespoons honey
  2 tablespoons vegetable oil

AT HOME:
Mix all ingredients except fruit and dry on a baking sheet in a 300°F. oven for 30 minutes, or until dry and browned. Stir every 8 or 10 minutes to prevent burning at edges. Cool, mix in fruit, and store in tins or plastic bags in a cool place. Makes 4 or 5 cups.

ON THE TRAIL:
Give each hiker a bag of mix for snacks.

TRAIL SNACKS

    1 lb. almonds, chopped
    1 lb. walnuts, chopped
    ¼ lb. sunflower seeds
    ¼ lb. dried apricots, chopped
    ½ lb. raisins
    ½ lb. dried pineapple, chopped
    ½ lb. banana chips
    ¼ lb. carob bits or M&Ms

AT HOME:
Toast nuts and seeds until lightly browned. Mix with dried fruits and carob or chocolate. Store in closed tins in a cool place.

ON THE TRAIL:
Give each hiker a plastic bag of mix for snacks.

VARIATIONS:
Mix 1 cup toasted soy nuts, 1 cup currants or raisins, 1 cup slivered almonds, and 1 12-oz. package M&Ms.

  Mix equal parts peanuts, sunflower seeds, chia seeds, walnuts, banana chips, dried apples, raisins, or apricots.

EDDY GORP

    10 oz. dates, pitted
     3 oz. dried apricots
     3 oz. currants
     3 oz. dark raisins
     4 oz. golden raisins
     3 oz. sesame seeds
     3 oz. sunflower seeds, shelled and toasted
     3 oz. pumpkin seeds, shelled and toasted
    12 oz. mixed nuts, salted

AT HOME:
Quarter dates lengthwise and roll in sesame seeds. Chop nuts. Mix all ingredients together and store in tins in a cool place.

ON THE TRAIL:
Give each hiker a plastic bag of mix for snacks or lunch.

> *Edith Ann Eddy*
> *Ithaca, New York*

KAIBAB GORP

    1 lb. M&Ms
    1 lb. granola
   12 oz. almonds *or* other nuts, roasted
    6 oz. dried apples
    6 oz. sunflower seeds, shelled and toasted

AT HOME:
Mix all ingredients together and store in tins in a cool place.

ON THE TRAIL:
Give each hiker a plastic bag of the mixture for trail snacks or lunch.

MARINATED FRUITS

    4 ounces dried fruits (apricots, pineapple,
           papaya, peaches, dates, *or* figs)
    1 cup sherry *or* white wine
   ½ cup whipped cream, *or* substitute

AT HOME:
Package fruit in plastic bag. Place wine and cream in separate plastic bottles. Keep cool.

IN CAMP:
Chop fruits into bite-size pieces. Marinate in sherry or white wine until soft. Serve topped with whipped cream. Serves two.

VARIATION:
Mix marinated fruits with vanilla or other instant pudding.

BOMBAY SCALLOPED APPLES

       3 oz. dried apples
    ⅛ teaspoon salt
       1 tablespoon lemon juice
    ⅛ teaspoon ginger
    ⅛ teaspoon curry powder
    ⅛ teaspoon dry mustard
       1 tablespoon butter
       1 tablespoon wheat germ
       1 oz. toasted slivered almonds
       1 oz. raisins
       1 tablespoon molasses

AT HOME:
Package apples in a plastic bag. Pour seasonings into a plastic bottle with molasses and butter. Package wheat germ, almonds, and raisins in three separate bags.

IN CAMP:
Soak apples in water to cover, about 15 minutes. Add all ingredients except almonds and raisins. Simmer until done, about 15 minutes. Stir in raisins and serve topped with almonds. Serve hot or cold. Serves two.

INDIAN FRUIT PUDDING

       5 tablespoons powdered eggs
       1 teaspoon salt
    ½ cup cornmeal
       4 tablespoons powdered milk
       1 cup cranberries *or* chopped figs *or* dates
    1½ cups water
       1 tablespoon butter

AT HOME:
Mix egg and salt with cornmeal and package in a plastic bag. Package milk in a second bag, and the fruits in a third.

IN CAMP:

Mix milk powder with water until dissolved. Melt butter in pot to coat bottom and sides. Pour milk into buttered pot and heat, but do not boil. Stir in cornmeal mixture. Cook 5 minutes, then mix in fruit. Cover and simmer on a low fire 15 minutes. Eat hot with honey, or cool overnight, slice, and fry for breakfast. Serves two.

RICE PUDDING

   ½ cup instant rice
   ⅓ cup raisins
   1 3¾-oz. package vanilla pudding (noninstant)
   1 cup powdered milk
   ¼ teaspoon cinnamon
   ⅛ teaspoon nutmeg
  2½ cups water

AT HOME:

Package rice and raisins in a plastic bag. Combine pudding, milk and seasonings in a second bag.

IN CAMP:

Pour rice and raisins into water, bring to a boil. Cook covered 5 to 10 minutes. Stir in milk and pudding mixture. Stir vigorously and cook until mixture begins to boil and lumps are dissolved. Makes 6 servings.

Judy O'Donnell
Lakewood, Colorado

RICE AND FIG PUDDING

  ¼ cup instant rice
  ½ cup figs, chopped
  ½ package vanilla pudding (3¾-oz. size)
  4 tablespoons powdered milk
  1 cup water

AT HOME:
Package rice and figs together in a plastic bag. Package powdered milk and vanilla pudding in a separate bag.

IN CAMP:
Bring water to a boil, add rice and figs and boil 2 or 3 minutes. Stir in powdered milk and pudding. Stir vigorously until lumps are dissolved and mixture is hot but not boiling. Remove from heat and set aside to cool. Serves two.

VARIATIONS:
Substitute pistachio pudding and raisins for vanilla pudding and figs.

Cook rice in pineapple juice instead of water. Add shredded coconut and grated ginger root instead of figs.

Soups & Sauces

✿ AVOCADO SOUP

2 ripe avocados
1 package chicken soup mix
1 tablespoon onion flakes
3 tablespoons powdered milk
½ cup sour cream
½ teaspoon salt
¼ teaspoon black pepper
1 cup water

AT HOME:
Package all dry ingredients in a plastic bag, the sour cream in a screw-top plastic jar, and the avocados (whole) in another plastic bag.

IN CAMP:
Add soup powder and onion flakes to water and bring to a boil. When dissolved, take off heat and let cool. Mash avocados. Stir powdered milk into 1 cup water, and add with sour cream, and avocados to soup. Add seasonings, heat briefly, but do not boil. Serve with a wedge of lemon. Serves two.

VARIATION:
Use 2 tablespoons bouillon powder, or 2 bouillon cubes. Soup may also be served cold.

BEAN SPROUT SOUP

1 package beef *or* chicken soup mix
1 tablespoon carrot flakes
1 tablespoon celery flakes
2 dried mushrooms, cut in pieces
1 teaspoon thyme leaves
½ teaspoon basil leaves
2 cloves garlic, minced
2 teaspoons soy sauce
1 cup bean sprouts, any kind
3 cups water

AT HOME:
Package soup mix and vegetable flakes in plastic bag together with mushrooms and seasonings. Package bean sprouts in a separate bag.

IN CAMP:
Add soup mix, vegetables, and seasonings to water and soak 10 minutes: Bring to a boil and simmer 10 or 15 minutes, until vegetables are soft. Add bean sprouts and heat 1 or 2 minutes. Add soy sauce to taste. Serves two.

✿ BEET SOUP

            2 medium beets
            1 tablespoon onion flakes
            2 oz. dried potato dices
            1 package chicken soup *or* 2 bouillon cubes
          ½ teaspoon salt
          ½ teaspoon black pepper
          ½ teaspoon dill weed
          ½ cup sour cream
            1 tablespoon lemon juice
            3 cups water

AT HOME:
Cook beets until tender, cool, slice thin and dry (see Beet Chips, p. 238). Package all vegetables in a plastic bag with seasonings. Package sour cream in a screw-top plastic jar.

IN CAMP:
Soak beets, onion flakes, potato dice, seasonings, and powdered soup in water for 15 minutes. Bring to a boil, simmer over low heat until vegetables are soft. Stir in sour cream and lemon juice. Serves two.

VARIATION:
Serve cold, topped with sour cream.

CHARD SOUP

    ½ lb. Swiss chard
    1 onion, minced, *or* 2 tablespoons onion flakes
    2 oz. potato dice *or* hash-browns (dried)
    2 tablespoons bacon bits
    2 chicken bouillon cubes
    1 teaspoon thyme leaves
    1 tablespoon butter
    ½ teaspoon salt
    ½ teaspoon black pepper
    3 cups water

AT HOME:
Wash and drain chard, pack in plastic bag. Package onion, potato, and bacon separately.

IN CAMP:
Chop chard leaves and slice stems into thin strips. Soak potatoes and bouillon in water while sautéeing onion in butter in pot. If onion flakes are used, soak in water with potatoes. Combine all ingredients except chard leaves and bacon bits, and bring to a boil. Simmer 10 minutes. Add chard leaves and simmer 5 minutes longer. Serve topped with bacon bits. Serves two.

CREAM OF CARROT SOUP

    2 carrots, *or* 2 oz. carrot flakes
    2 oz. potato dice *or* hash-browns (dried)
    2 tablespoons celery flakes
    1 tablespoon onion flakes
    2 chicken bouillon cubes
    1 teaspoon marjoram leaves *or* thyme
    ½ teaspoon salt
    ¼ teaspoon black pepper
    1 cup milk
    2 cups water

AT HOME:
Package all vegetable flakes, bouillon and seasonings together. Wash carrots and package in plastic bag with paper towel to absorb moisture and keep carrots fresh.

IN CAMP:
Add vegetables to water and soak 15 minutes. Slice carrots into thin rounds and add to other vegetables. Bring to a boil, add seasonings, and simmer 15 minutes or until vegetables are soft. Stir in milk and heat, but do not boil. Serves two.

CHEESE SOUP

  1 cup grated Cheddar, Parmesan *or* Romano cheese
3–4 bouillon cubes
  2 oz. potato flakes
  1 tablespoon parsley, dried *or* fresh
  1 teaspoon marjoram leaves *or* dill weed
  1 teaspoon salt
  ½ teaspoon black pepper
  3 cups water

AT HOME:
Grate and package cheese in plastic bag. Package bouillon, potato flakes, and seasonings in a separate plastic bag.

IN CAMP:
Add bouillon, potato flakes, and seasonings to water and mix well. Add cheese and heat until cheese is melted. Serve with Rye Pretzels (p. 115). Serves two.

CHINESE WONTON SOUP

  2 packages wonton soup mix with pork
  1 package (1 oz.) freeze-dried peas
  1 package (1 oz.) dried shrimp
  2 teaspoons soy sauce
  3 cups boiling water

AT HOME:
Package ingredients in separate plastic bags.

IN CAMP:
Add shrimp and wonton to water and let simmer 5 minutes. Add peas, simmer 1 minute longer. Add soy sauce to taste. Serves two.

Irene Reti
Los Angeles, California

CLAM SOUP

   1 7-oz. can minced clams
   1 medium cucumber
   2 green onions
 ½ small green bell pepper
   1 sprig parsley
   1 tablespoon horseradish
 ½ teaspoon salt
   2 tablespoons powdered milk
   3 cups water

AT HOME:
Wash vegetables and package in plastic bag with a paper towel to absorb moisture and keep vegetables fresh.

IN CAMP:
Peel and chop cucumber. Chop onions, pepper, and parsley fine. Add all vegetables except parsley to water, bring to a boil, and simmer 15 minutes. Add clams and cook until well heated. Make a paste of milk and a little water. Add milk to soup and simmer 3 or 4 minutes, but do not let boil. Garnish soup with parsley, and serve with Cobblestone Crackers (p. 111). Serves two.

CURRIED CREAM OF PEA SOUP

2½ oz. freeze-dried peas
1 tablespoon onion flakes
1 tablespoon celery flakes
1 tablespoon carrot flakes
2 oz. potato dice *or* hash-browns (dried)
2 chicken bouillon cubes
1 clove garlic, minced
1 tablespoon curry powder
2 tablespoons powdered milk
½ teaspoon salt
1 tablespoon parsley flakes, *or* fresh parsley
3 cups water

AT HOME:
Package all ingredients in a plastic bag with seasonings, except milk, parsley, and peas, which should be packaged in separate bags.

IN CAMP:
Add vegetables and bouillon to water and soak for 15 minutes. Bring to a boil and simmer 10 minutes. Mix milk into a paste with a little water and stir into soup. Do not let boil. Serve topped with minced parsley. Serves two.

CURRIED MUSHROOMS TOP RAMEN

1 oz. dried mushrooms, sliced
2 packages Top Ramen noodles (beef, pork,
        or chicken flavor)
1 package curry sauce mix *or* 3 tablespoons curry powder
4 cups water

AT HOME:
Package ingredients in separate plastic bags.

In camp:
Slice mushrooms and soak in water 15 minutes. Add noodles and curry powder and boil for three minutes. Serves four.

Marcella Kemsley
White Plains, New York

CREAM OF MUSHROOM SOUP

  1 package mushroom soup
  2 tablespoons celery flakes
  2 tablespoons onion flakes
  2 tablespoons powdered milk
  2 tablespoons parsley flakes
  3 cups water

At home:
Package all ingredients except milk in a plastic bag. Package milk in a second bag.

In camp:
Add soup and vegetables to water. Soak for 10 minutes and bring to a boil. Simmer 5 minutes. Mix a bit of cold water with milk and stir into soup mixture. Heat, but do not permit to boil. Serves two.

Variations:
Add 4 tablespoons dried spinach flakes at the beginning of soaking time.
    Add a 6-oz. can of chicken to soup mixture and heat before adding milk.

CREAMED CHIPPED SOUP

  1 3-oz. package chipped beef
  1 1½-oz. package cream of mushroom soup
  ⅓ cup powdered milk
  2 stalks celery, chopped fine
  1½ cups water

AT HOME:
Wash and trim celery and package in a plastic bag with a paper towel to absorb moisture. Package soup and milk together.

IN CAMP:
Chop celery fine. Chop chipped beef and rinse to remove excess salt. Mix soup and milk with water until smooth. Add chipped beef and chopped celery. Heat until steaming, stirring constantly. Serve over toast, rice, or noodles. Serves three.

Judy Hirsch
Santa Ana, California

JERKY SOUP

    3 beef bouillon cubes
    5 sticks of beef jerky
    1 cup shell macaroni
    1 tablespoon parsley leaves
    1 tablespoon basil, oregano, *or* other herbs
    3 cups water

AT HOME:
Break jerky into small pieces and package in plastic bag with macaroni and seasonings.

IN CAMP:
Add bouillon to water and bring to a boil. Add macaroni and jerky and let simmer 15 minutes, stirring occasionally, until macaroni is done and jerky softened. Serves two.

David Sorric
Santa Paula, California

MEATBALL SOUP

      8 meatballs, freeze-dried *or* home-dried
      2 beef bouillon cubes
      1 tablespoon tomato concentrate
      2 tablespoons onion flakes
      1 tablespoon carrot flakes
      2 oz. potato dice *or* hash-browns (dried)
      1 clove garlic, minced
      1 tablespoon oregano leaves
      1 teaspoon cayenne
      2 tablespoons butter
    1–2 tablespoons parsley leaves, minced
      3 cups water

AT HOME:
Prepare tomato concentrate (p. 240) and meatballs (p. 242 if home-dried are used). Package meatballs, tomato concentrate, and vegetables in a plastic bag with seasonings.

IN CAMP:
Add all ingredients to water and soak 15 minutes. Bring to a boil, add butter and simmer 10 minutes. Serve topped with parsley. Serves two.

MUSHROOM SOY SOUP

      2 packages instant cream of mushroom soup mix
    ½ cup mixed dried vegetables
    ½ cup dry textured soy protein, any flavor (TVP)
      2 tablespoons butter
    ¼ teaspoon salt
    ¼ teaspoon pepper
      4 cups boiling water

AT HOME:
Package all dry ingredients except vegetables in a plastic bag; package vegetables in a separate bag.

IN CAMP:

Soak dried vegetables in a cup of water until liquid is absorbed, about 20 minutes. Add vegetables to boiling water and cook about 5 minutes. Mix in textured vegetable protein and mushroom soup mix, let stand 5 minutes. Add butter and seasonings. Serves two.

> *Kathy Linet*
> *Northridge, California*

HOT FRUIT SOUP

    ¼ cup raisins
    ½ cup dried prunes
    ½ cup dried apples
    ¼ cup mixed dried fruits (pears, peaches)
    ⅛ teaspoon salt
    ¼ cup Tang breakfast drink
    1 small package raspberry gelatin
    1 cinnamon stick
    ½ cup instant coffee creamer *or* powdered milk
    1 cup hot water
    ¼ cup shredded coconut

AT HOME:

Package all fruits together in plastic bag. Package Tang and gelatin in a bag together with cinnamon stick. Package instant creamer and shredded coconut in separate bags.

IN CAMP:

Soak dried fruit for an hour. Add salt, Tang, gelatin powder and cinnamon stick. Bring to a boil, cover, and simmer 15 minutes, or until fruit is tender. Dissolve creamer or milk in hot water and add to fruit. Top servings with coconut. Serves four.

> *Kathleen Sykes*
> *Missoula, Montana*

GARLIC SOUP

  6 large cloves garlic, minced
  3 tablespoons powdered beef bouillon *or* 4 cubes
  4 tablespoons grated Parmesan cheese
  2 slices bread
  2 tablespoons butter
½ cup sherry
  3 cups water

AT HOME:
Package ingredients separately in plastic bags. Pour sherry into plastic bottle.

IN CAMP:
Add minced garlic and bouillon to water and bring to a boil. Simmer about 10 minutes. Toast bread, butter it, and place in soup bowls. Add sherry to soup and heat 1 minute. Pour soup over toast and top with cheese. Serves two.

LENTIL SOUP MADRID

½ cup precooked dried lentils
  1 tablespoon tomato concentrate
  1 tablespoon onion, minced
  1 tablespoon green pepper, minced
  3 tablespoons pimiento (canned), diced
  2 tablespoons celery, diced
  1 clove garlic, minced
  2 tablespoons olive oil
½ teaspoon salt
  1 teaspoon cayenne
  3 cups water

AT HOME:
Precook and dry lentils (p. 238). Prepare tomato concentrate (p. 240). Package lentils and tomato concentrate in plastic bag. Wash vegetables and package in plastic bag.

IN CAMP:
Soak lentils with tomato concentrate in water 15 minutes. Add vegetables and olive oil and simmer 15 minutes. Add seasonings. Serves two.

VARIATION:
Add one chopped, sautéed chorizo (Mexican sausage) while mixture is simmering.

SPROUTED LENTIL SOUP

> 1 package onion soup mix
> 1 cup sprouted lentils
> 3 cups water

AT HOME:
Cut a hole in a plastic jug halfway down the side opposite the handle. Pour in 2 or 3 tablespoons lentils. Soak overnight and drain.

ON THE TRAIL:
Sprinkle the lentils with water several times during the day to keep them moist. After two to four days, the sprouts will be ready to eat.

IN CAMP:
Mix soup powder with water and bring to a boil. Just before serving, add 1 cup lentil sprouts. Serves two.

> *Cindy Campbell*
> *Gainesville, Florida*

POTATO SOUP

> 4 oz. hash-brown potato dice (dried)
> 1 tablespoon onion flakes
> 1 tablespoon celery flakes
> 1 tablespoon dill weed
> 1 tablespoon parsley flakes
> ½ teaspoon cloves
> ½ teaspoon salt
> ¼ teaspoon black pepper
> 3 cups water
> 2 tablespoons butter

AT HOME:
Mix dry ingredients together and package in a plastic bag.

IN CAMP:
Add dry ingredients to water and soak for 10 or 15 minutes. Add butter and bring to a boil. Simmer for 10 minutes. Serves two.

BASQUE POTATO SOUP

> 4 oz. Italian sausage
> 2 oz. potato flakes
> 2 tablespoons onion flakes
> 1 tablespoon tomato concentrate (p. 240)
> 2 beef bouillon cubes
> 1 tablespoon celery flakes
> 1 tablespoon parsley flakes
> ½ teaspoon thyme leaves
> 1 bay leaf
> 1 teaspoon salt
> 1 tablespoon lemon juice
> ¼ teaspoon black pepper
> 3 cups water

AT HOME:
Package all dry ingredients together in a plastic bag. Package sausage separately.

IN CAMP:
Slice sausage and brown in bottom of pot over medium heat. Add water and dry ingredients and soak 15 minutes. Bring to a boil, add lemon juice, and simmer 15 minutes. Serves two.

INSTANT POTATO SOUP

> 1 cup instant potato flakes
> ¾ cup powdered milk
> ½ teaspoon onion powder
> ½ teaspoon garlic powder
> 1 tablespoon parsley flakes
> ½ teaspoon curry powder
> ½ teaspoon dill weed
> ¼ teaspoon Italian seasoning
> ¼ teaspoon black pepper
> 1 tablespoon butter

AT HOME:
Mix all ingredients except butter and package in plastic bag.

IN CAMP:
Add butter and 2–4 tablespoons of potato mixture to each cup of hot water, depending on thickness desired.

Lynna Walker
Los Angeles, California

PEANUT BUTTER SOUP

> 2 tablespoons peanut butter, or more
> 2 chicken *or* vegetable bouillon cubes
> 1 package (1½ or 2 oz.) Oriental noodles
> 3 cups water

AT HOME:
Package peanut butter in a screw-top plastic jar. Package noodles in a plastic bag with bouillon.

IN CAMP:
Add noodles and bouillon to boiling water and boil for 2 minutes. Mix peanut butter with a little water to form a thin paste and pour into soup, mixing well. Serves two.

SENEGALESE SOUP

   1 7-oz. can chicken *or* 3 oz. freeze-dried chicken
   2 tablespoons onion flakes
   2 tablespoons celery flakes
   1 apple, chopped finely
   1 tablespoon curry powder
   2 tablespoons butter
   1 bay leaf
   2 tablespoons powdered milk
   3 cups water

AT HOME:
Mix all dry ingredients except milk and package in plastic bag.

IN CAMP:
Add all ingredients except milk to water and bring to a boil. Simmer 15 minutes, and remove bay leaf. Mix milk with a little water to form a paste, and stir into soup. Heat 3 or 4 minutes, but do not boil. Serves two.

TOMATO-BOUILLON SOUP

    1 cup tomato juice, V-8 *or* similar juice
1–2 bouillon cubes; vegetable, beef *or* chicken
    1 tablespoon parsley, celery flakes, basil
              or thyme leaves, as desired
    1 cup water

AT HOME:
Package bouillon and any seasonings to be used in 35mm. film cans, or plastic bottles.

IN CAMP:
Bring water to a boil and dissolve bouillon. Add tomato juice and seasonings, and stir over medium heat until steaming. Serves two.

Mary Belcher
Memphis, Tennessee

TOMATO CELERY SOUP

   1 package dried tomato soup
   2 stalks celery, chopped finely
   4 tablespoons Parmesan cheese, grated
   3 cups water

AT HOME:
Wash, trim, and chop celery, and package in a plastic bag with paper towel to absorb moisture and keep celery fresh.

IN CAMP:
Mix soup and celery into water and bring to a boil. Simmer about 10 minutes. Celery should remain crisp. Top with Parmesan cheese and serve with Whole Wheat Crackers (p. 114). Serves two.

SOUP TO NUTS

   1 package (2 oz.) noodle soup with chicken broth
   3 oz. spinach noodles
   ¾ cup instant rice
   1 tablespoon chicken bouillon powder
   ¾ cup toasted slivered almonds
   ¾ cup raisins
   4 cups water

AT HOME:
Package noodles, soup, instant rice, and bouillon in one plastic bag. Package almonds and raisins in a second bag.

In camp:
Add contents of soup and noodle bag to boiling water. Boil 8 minutes. Stir in raisins and almonds and heat. Makes 5 cups.

Jim Tingey
Northbrook, Illinois

ZUCCHINI SOUP

> 2 medium zucchini
> 2 tablespoons butter
> 2 chicken bouillon cubes
> 1 tablespoon oregano leaves *or* basil leaves
> 2 tablespoons powdered milk
> 1 teaspoon salt
> ¼ teaspoon black pepper
> 3 cups water
> 2 tablespoons Parmesan *or* Romano cheese, grated

At home:
Wash zucchini and package in plastic bag. Package seasonings and powdered milk in one plastic bag, and grated cheese in another.

In camp:
Slice or chop zucchini fine. Add to water with butter and bouillon cubes, and bring to a boil. Simmer 10 minutes. Add seasonings and milk, mixed with water to form a paste. Heat 2 or 3 minutes, but do not boil. Serve topped with Parmesan cheese or Romano cheese, grated. Serves two.

Variation:
Substitute 1 tablespoon tomato concentrate (p. 240) for milk to create a tomato-zucchini soup.

> ## SAUCES
>
> Some sauces may be prepared from soup powders, thickened just enough with milk or water, and heated to the proper consistency.
>
> Other sauces may be prepared at home and packaged in plastic screw-top jars, chilled, and taken along for use in camp. (See p. 51 for cooling and transporting perishable ingredients.)
>
> AT HOME:
> Prepare ingredients necessary for the sauce needed for a particular recipe to be prepared in camp. Package all the ingredients according to the recipes.
>
> IN CAMP:
> Prepare each sauce according to the recipe or use.

CASHEW SAUCE FOR WALNUT-OAT PATTIES

    ½ cup cashew nut pieces
    2 tablespoons arrowroot *or* cornstarch
    ½ teaspoon salt
    2 tablespoons onion powder
  1–2 tablespoons soy sauce
    2 tablespoons margarine, melted
    2 cups water

AT HOME:
Pulverize cashews in blender or with rolling pin. Mix with other dry ingredients and package in a plastic bag.

IN CAMP:
Add water to dry ingredients and margarine and mix to form a smooth paste. Simmer, stirring constantly to prevent lumps. When

the mixture is a medium thick sauce, pour over Walnut-Oat Patties (p. 216).

Joe Sweeney
Salem, New Hampshire

CHILE SAUCE FOR CHARQUI CON CHILE

  2 lbs. dried chile pods *or*
         1 package (10 oz.) frozen red chiles
  1 8-oz. can tomato sauce
  ½ teaspoon cilantro (coriander) leaves, crushed
  1 tablespoon oregano leaves, crushed
3½ cups water
  2 tablespoons flour *or* cornmeal

AT HOME:
Wash chile pods and toast for 2 minutes in a 350°F. oven. Remove stems and seeds, purée in blender with a little water. Combine with tomato sauce, cilantro (coriander), oregano, and water. Simmer 20 minutes, stirring occasionally. Add flour or cornmeal to thicken sauce, and cook 2 or 3 minutes longer. Marinate Charqui con Chile (p. 243) in the sauce.

Benny Sena, Sr.
Las Animas, Colorado

CHICKEN SAUCE

  ½ onion
  5 mushrooms
  1 tablespoon butter or oil
  1 package sour cream sauce

IN CAMP:
Sauté onion and mushrooms, sliced thin, in oil or butter. Mix sour cream sauce powder with enough water to form a paste and add to sautéed vegetables. Cook over low flame until a medium-

thick sauce is formed. Add more water if needed. When cooked, pour over broiled or boiled chicken and serve. Serves two.

✹ CREAM SAUCE

2 tablespoons mayonnaise
1½ tablespoons flour
¼ teaspoon salt
4 tablespoons milk powder
1 cup water

IN CAMP:

Cook mayonnaise and flour together briefly. Add milk powder and salt mixed with 1 cup water, and stir over low heat until sauce thickens to proper consistency. Makes 1¼ cups sauce.

MUSHROOM SAUCE

½ package mushroom soup
½ cup water
1 tablespoon butter or oil
 vegetable flakes (optional)
 herbs (optional)

IN CAMP:

Mix soup powder with water, add butter or oil and heat. Add parsley leaves, basil leaves, chives, or other herbs, or onion flakes, celery flakes, pepper flakes, for additional seasoning, to taste. Serve over eggs and ham, open-face sandwiches, or meats. Serves two.

PESTO

2 cups fresh basil leaves
2 or 3 cloves garlic
3 sprigs parsley
½ cup olive oil
½ teaspoon salt
1 cup Romano or Parmesan cheese, grated

AT HOME:
Chop basil, garlic, and parsley. Mix with olive oil, salt, and cheese. Store in refrigerator. Keeps a week or two. Package in plastic screw-top bottle for camping trip.

IN CAMP:
Add 3 tablespoons pesto to ½ cup (1 stick) soft butter for ⅔ cup Pesto Butter. Serve on cooked vegetables, baked potatoes, in soup, or mixed with breadcrumbs to top broiled tomatoes. Mix with noodles or other cooked pastas.

✿ SOUR CREAM SUBSTITUTE

½ cup small-curd cottage cheese
¼ cup plain yoghurt
2–3 tablespoons milk

AT HOME:
Mix together to a smooth consistency in blender. Add more milk if needed. Package in plastic screw-top jar and keep chilled.

IN CAMP:
Use sauce for cabbage salads, to top eggs or vegetables and any other food for which sour cream is used.

✿ TARTAR SAUCE

½ cup mayonnaise
2 green onions, chopped
2 tablespoons pickle relish
dash of Tabasco sauce

AT HOME:
Mix together ingredients and package in a plastic screw-top jar for camp. Keep cool.

IN CAMP:
Use sauce for broiled or grilled fish.

Cereals, Grains, & Pastas

CORNMEAL MUSH

½ cup yellow cornmeal
⅔ cup instant powdered milk
2 tablespoons soy flour (optional)
½ teaspoon salt
2 cups water
1–2 eggs (optional)

AT HOME:
Mix dry ingredients together in a plastic bag and label.

IN CAMP:
Make a smooth paste of dry ingredients and ½ cup water. Add paste slowly to 1½ cups boiling water, stirring constantly until mixture is thick, about 10 minutes. Remove from heat, stir in eggs and whatever condiments the situation demands. Serves two.

Byron Robitaille
Charlottesville, Virginia

MARYLAND SCRAPPLE

½ lb. pork sausage
½ teaspoon sage
½ teaspoon thyme
½ teaspoon salt
1 pint boiling water
½ cup cornmeal

AT HOME:
Add sausage to seasoned boiling water and stir to break up lumps. Pour in cornmeal, stirring constantly to avoid lumps. Lower heat, cover, and cook slowly 40 minutes, stirring frequently. Pour into plastic cartons (round ice cream cartons are good) and freeze. Place cartons in plastic bags, keep cool.

IN CAMP:

Slice into ½" thick slices and fry. Serves two or three. Serve with eggs or with butter and syrup.

VARIATION:

Take along frozen sausage, packaged seasoned cornmeal, and make at night in camp. Let chill overnight, slice and fry for breakfast.

✿ FRESH FRUIT AND CEREAL

    ½ cup rolled oats
    ½ cup ground walnuts
    1 cup yoghurt
    1 tablespoon honey
      juice of 2 lemons
    1 quart fruit *or* berries in season

AT HOME:

Mix nuts and oatmeal and package in plastic bag. Mix honey with yoghurt in a screw-top plastic container. Wash fruit and package separately.

IN CAMP:

Slice fruit and cover with lemon juice; add yoghurt and dry ingredients and mix well. Serves five or six.

Greg Poole
Setauket, New York

CHOCOLATE OATMEAL

    1 envelope instant hot chocolate mix
    1 envelope instant oatmeal, any flavor
    1 cup hot water

IN CAMP:
Mix together for a quick breakfast and enjoy.

Karen L. Northeimer
Stevens, Pennsylvania

MINCEMEAT OATMEAL

   9 oz. condensed mincemeat
18 oz. quick-cooking oats
   1 quart powdered milk (optional)

AT HOME:
Package a 9-oz. block of condensed mincemeat and 18 oz. quick oats separately in 9 plastic bags for 9 servings. If desired, add 1 quart powdered milk to oatmeal, for additional nutrition.

IN CAMP:
Add 1 oz. of mincemeat to $1\frac{1}{2}$ cups salted water and bring to a boil. Add 2 oz. oatmeal to water, stirring constantly. Cook one minute. Serves one.

Edward G. Menard
North Kingston, Rhode Island

GRAPE-NUTS AND FRUIT

   3 oz. Grape-Nuts
$\frac{1}{2}$ cup chopped dates, papaya, pineapple,
          banana flakes, *or* other dried fruit
   4 oz. powdered milk
   2 cups water

AT HOME:
Chop fruit and package with Grape-Nuts in a plastic bag.

IN CAMP:

Mix milk powder with 2 cups water for double-strength milk for cereal. *Or,* add milk powder to cereal and fruit and mix with hot water for a hot cereal on a cold morning. Serves two.

CAMP CEREAL

>   1 cup cracked wheat
>   1 cup rolled wheat
>   ¼ cup brown sugar
>   ½ cup dried chopped apples
>   ½ cup raisins

AT HOME:

Mix all ingredients in plastic bag and label.

IN CAMP:

Pour half mixture in a pot and cover with water. Let stand overnight. Next morning, add just enough water to keep cereal from sticking to the pot and heat, stirring occasionally. Serves two, for two meals.

VARIATION:

Use dried papaya or pineapple instead of apples.

>   *Diana Ashby-Bigelow*
>   *Iowa City, Iowa*

EASY GRANOLA

>   5 cups old-fashioned oats
>   1 cup chopped apple
>   1 cup chopped pecans
>   ¼ cup melted butter
>   ¼ cup brown sugar
>   1½ teaspoons cinnamon
>   ½ cup raisins (optional)

AT HOME:
Toast oats on ungreased cookie sheet in a 350°F. oven for 10 to 12 minutes. Combine oats with other ingredients and mix well. Spread mixture on cookie sheet and bake in a 350°F. oven for 35 minutes, stirring occasionally. Cool, and store in oatmeal boxes in refrigerator until needed. Makes 9 cups.

Tina Dodson
Bonne Terre, Missouri

GRANOLA

    5 cups rolled oats
    1 cup slivered almonds
    1 cup sesame seeds
    1 cup sunflower seeds
    1 cup shredded coconut
    1 cup powdered milk
    1 cup soy flour
    1 cup wheat germ
    1 cup honey
    1 cup vegetable oil
 1–2 cups dried fruit (chopped dates, figs,
            apples, currants)

AT HOME:
Mix all dry ingredients except fruit. Add honey and oil and mix well. Spread on two cookie sheets and bake in a 250°F. oven for 1 hour, stirring every 10 minutes. Add fruit, let cool, and store in tins in refrigerator until needed. Makes 3 quarts.

Lucille I. Collins
East Aurora, New York

SUN CLOUD GRANOLA

    3 cups rolled oats
    1 cup rolled wheat
    2 cups coconut, shredded
    ½ cup wheat germ
    ½ cup sunflower seeds
    ½ cup sesame seeds
    ½ cup soy grits
    ½ cup bran
    ½ cup pumpkin seeds
    1 cup cashews, chopped
    1 cup walnuts, chopped
    ⅔ cup oil—safflower or other
    1 cup honey
    3 teaspoons vanilla
    1 cup chopped dates
    2 cups raisins *or* other dried fruits, chopped

AT HOME:
Mix liquid ingredients with dry ingredients, except fruit. Spread in baking tins and brown in a 250°F. oven for about 40 minutes, stirring often. Cool, add fruit, and store in tins in the refrigerator until needed.

Sarah Kemsley
Cheshire, Oregon

WALNUT-OAT PATTIES WITH CASHEW SAUCE

    1 cup whole wheat breadcrumbs
    ½ teaspoon basil
    ½ teaspoon tarragon
    ½ teaspoon thyme
    1 cup quick oats
    1 cup (3 oz.) finely chopped walnuts
    ¼ cup soy flour
    1 teaspoon salt
    2 tablespoons peanut *or* cashew butter (optional)
      oil or margarine

AT HOME:
Season breadcrumbs with herbs. Package all dry ingredients in plastic bag and label. Package nut butter in a screw-top plastic jar.

IN CAMP:
Add to the oat and breadcrumb mixture enough nut butter and water to hold mixture together. Form into patties and sauté in oil or margarine. Makes two 8-oz. patties or four 4-oz. patties. Serve topped with Cashew Sauce (p. 204). Serves two.

Joe Sweeney
Salem, New Hamsphire

BULGUR, BULGHUR, or BURGHUL as the Arabs call it, has long been a Middle Eastern staple. Whole wheat grains are parboiled and dried, the bran is removed, and the kernels are cracked into fine, medium, coarse or whole particles. Parboiling precooks the wheat. "Fine grind" bulgur needs only be rehydrated and warmed to be ready to eat.

Stocked on supermarket shelves as "Ala," bulgur may be purchased in health-food stores, ethnic groceries, or stores where grains are sold in bulk. The rich, nutty flavor combines well with fruits, vegetables, cheeses, fish, and meat. Bulgur may be eaten hot or cold.

FOR PREPARATION:
Two parts of water are required to one part of grain; ½ cup of grain will make about 2 cups of reconstituted bulgur.

BULGUR WITH FRUIT AND NUTS

1 cup finely ground bulgur
1 teaspoon salt
2 cups water
½ cup nuts, raisins *or* berries

AT HOME:
Package bulgur in plastic bag and label.

IN CAMP:
Add salt to water and bring to a boil. Stir in bulgur, nuts, raisins, and other fruit. Lower heat, cover, and cook for 1 minute. Remove from heat and let stand 5 to 10 minutes. Serve with brown sugar and milk. Serves two.

> *Kathy Hope*
> *Seattle, Washington*

TABBOULI I (*Bulgur Salad*)

      1 cup bulgur wheat
    6–8 green onions
      1 green pepper
      1 cucumber
      1 tomato
      1 clove garlic, minced
      1 tablespoon mint leaves
    ½ cup olive *or* other vegetable oil
    ¼ cup lemon juice
        salt and pepper to taste
      2 cups water

AT HOME:
Wash, trim, and package all vegetables wrapped in damp paper towels in plastic bags. Package bulgur wheat in a separate bag.

IN CAMP:
Chop all vegetables fine. Cover bulgur wheat with 2 cups boiling water and let soak 1 or 1½ hours until wheat is softened. Mix in all other ingredients and let set 10 or 15 minutes while flavors meld. Scoop up mixture on romaine lettuce leaves or celery stalks. Serves three or four. Use any combination of raw vegetables.

> *Laura Wright*
> *Summit, New Jersey*

✿ TABBOULI II

   ½ cup bulgur wheat
   2 tablespoons sunflower seeds
   2 tablespoons sesame seeds
   6 green onions, chopped fine
   3 cloves garlic, minced
   1 tablespoon ginger root, grated or minced
   1 cup boiling water
   1 tablespoon lemon juice
   2 tablespoons sour cream *or* olive oil

IN CAMP:

Mix seeds, garlic, and ginger root with wheat and pour boiling water on mixture. Let stand 1 hour, or until wheat is soft. Mix in vegetables, lemon juice, and olive oil or sour cream. Serve with leaves of romaine lettuce or Chinese (nappa) cabbage as scoops or servers. Serves two.

VARIATION:

Add 1 diced tomato, 1 cucumber, peeled and diced, and 2 sprigs of parsley instead of seeds. Use Chinese parsley leaves (coriander) instead of ginger root.

GREEN MOUNTAIN STEW

   ¾ cup bulgur
   ¾ cup freeze-dried peas
   1 5-oz. can Vienna sausage
   3 cups water

AT HOME:

Package bulgur and peas in a plastic bag and label.

IN CAMP:

Add bulgur and peas to water and bring to a boil. Let simmer 10 to 15 minutes until water is absorbed. Add sausages 5 minutes before cooking is over, and stir. Serve with butter and salt. Serves two.

Laura and Guy Waterman
East Corinth, Vermont

BULGUR STEW

    ¾ cup bulgur
    1 package instant tomato soup
    1 package instant onion soup
    ¼ cup powdered milk
    2 oz. grated cheese, any kind
    3 tablespoons sunflower *or* sesame seeds
    1 teaspoon garlic powder
    1 teaspoon salt
    2 cups water

AT HOME:
Package all dry ingredients in plastic bag. Package cheese and seeds in separate plastic bags.

IN CAMP:
Bring water to a boil and add dry ingredients. Lower heat, cover, and cook about 20 minutes. Stir in cheese and seeds. Serves two.

VARIATION:
Add chopped vegetables for a heartier stew.

    Alan Miller
    Durango, Colorado

PEMIGEWASSET STEW

    ¾ cup millet
    ¼ cup precooked dried garbanzo beans (chickpeas)
    ¾ cup dehydrated mixed vegetables
    4 tablespoons margarine
    1 teaspoon salt
    3½ cups water

AT HOME:
Package all ingredients except margarine in a plastic bag. Package margarine in a plastic screw-top jar, or take along a bottle of margarine, 1-lb. size.

IN CAMP:

Add all ingredients to water and bring to a boil. Cook until mixture is tender and water is absorbed, about 15 minutes. Serves two.

> *Laura and Guy Waterman*
> *East Corinth, Vermont*

WHITE MOUNTAIN STEW

¾ cup couscous*
¼ cup black-eyed peas
¾ cup dehydrated mixed vegetables
3 tablespoons butter
½ teaspoon salt
3½ cups water

AT HOME:

Package vegetables and peas together in plastic bag. Package couscous separately. Store butter in plastic jar with screw-top lid.

IN CAMP:

Add black-eyed peas and vegetables, butter, and salt to water. Bring to a boil and cook until vegetables are tender, about 15 minutes. Add couscous and cook 5 minutes longer. Serves two.

> *Laura and Guy Waterman*
> *East Corinth, Vermont*

---

* Couscous consists of tiny pellets of cracked wheat used in North African cooking. It may be found in health-food stores. The couscous and black-eyed peas combine to make a complete protein.

WEETAMOO STEW

          1 cup quick rice
        ½ cup bulgur
        ¼ cup cashew pieces
          1 package cream of mushroom soup
          2 tablespoons dried green vegetables
        ¼ cup dried mushrooms
          1 teaspoon garlic powder
          1 teaspoon salt
        ½ teaspoon pepper
          2 tablespoons butter or margarine
          4 cups water

AT HOME:
Combine all dry ingredients in a plastic bag. Pack butter or margarine in a plastic container.

IN CAMP:
Add all ingredients to water and bring to a boil. Simmer 15 to 20 minutes. Serves four.

VARIATION:
Dried beef or tuna may be added.

Bill Rogers
Groton, Connecticut

RAISIN RICE CEREAL

        ½ cup instant rice
        ½ cup raisins
          1 tablespoon butter
        ½ teaspoon salt
       2½ cups water

AT HOME:
Package rice and raisins in plastic bag and label.

IN CAMP:
Add butter and salt to water and bring to a boil. Stir in rice and raisins and cook, stirring constantly, for 2 minutes. Remove from heat, cover, and let stand 5 to 10 minutes. Serve with milk and a topping of honey, shredded coconut, nuts, or banana flakes. Serves two.

✿ ARROZ CON CHILES

    4 oz. quick or instant rice
    1 4-oz. can green chiles, diced
    4 oz. Jack or Cheddar cheese, diced
    2 oz. sour cream *or* 1 package (2 oz.) dried sour cream sauce
    ¼ cup Parmesan cheese, grated
    1 tablespoon butter
    ¼ teaspoon salt
    1 cup water

IN CAMP:
Add rice and all ingredients except sour cream and Parmesan cheese to water and bring to a boil. Simmer 15 to 20 minutes, or until rice is done. If instant rice is used, boil briefly and set aside 10 minutes to absorb water. Stir in sour cream and serve topped with Parmesan cheese. Serves two.

VARIATION:
Add 2 oz. freeze-dried or 4 oz. canned chicken per person for a heartier meal.

GREEN RICE

    4 oz. rice
    2 tablespoons chicken bouillon powder
    3 tablespoons parsley flakes
    3 green onions, minced
    2 tablespoons green pepper flakes
    2 tablespoons butter
    ½ teaspoon salt
    1½ cups water

AT HOME:
Package all dry ingredients in a plastic bag.

IN CAMP:
Add all ingredients to salted boiling water and bring back to a boil. Cover and simmer 15 or 20 minutes, until rice is done and water is absorbed. If instant rice is used, boil briefly, about 1 minute, and set aside 10 minutes to absorb water. Serves two.

VARIATIONS:
Add canned chicken, shrimp or clams to mixture before cooking.
  Add chopped olives and olive oil or sour cream and serve cold, as a salad.
  Add 2 oz. dried mushrooms to mixture before cooking.
  Add chopped ham, bacon bar, or Vienna sausages before cooking.

✿ RICE WITH CUCUMBERS

         4 oz. instant rice
         1 tablespoon butter
         2 teaspoons soy sauce
           water
         2 cucumbers, peeled and chopped
         2 green onions, chopped
         2 teaspoons basil
         1 teaspoon cayenne
         1 teaspoon salt (optional)
         3 tablespoons sour cream
       1½ cups boiling water

AT HOME:
Package rice in a plastic bag. Package vegetables in a plastic bag with a damp paper towel.

IN CAMP:
Add butter and soy to boiling water and pour in rice. Mix in chopped cucumbers, onions, and seasonings. Boil briefly and set aside for 10 minutes, until rice is soft and water absorbed. Serve topped with sour cream. Serves two.

CASHEW RICE CURRY

    ¼ cup powdered milk
    1 cup converted rice
    ¼ cup cashew nut pieces
    2 oz. grated Cheddar cheese *or* mozzarella
  1–2 teaspoons curry powder
    ½ teaspoon salt
    3 cups water

AT HOME:
Package milk, rice, and other ingredients in separate plastic bags and label.

IN CAMP:
Mix milk and seasonings with a little water to form a paste. Add the rest of the water, mix well, and bring to a boil. Stir in rice, cover, and simmer until the liquid is absorbed and rice is soft, about 20 minutes. Stir in nuts and cheese; let stand until cheese has melted. Serves two or three.

Spencer E. Schwinhart
Frostburg, Maryland

CURRIED VEGETABLES

    1 2-oz. package vegetable soup mix
  2½ cups water
    1 cup instant rice
    1 tablespoon curry powder
    3 oz. raisins
    2 oz. nuts
    1 oz. shredded coconut

AT HOME:
Package all ingredients in separate plastic bags and label.

IN CAMP:
Add vegetable soup mix to water and bring to a boil. Add rice
and stir. Add curry powder, raisins, and nuts and mix well. Cover
pot and let stand 10 minutes until rice is soft. Sprinkle coconut on
top. Serves two.

F. Story Clark
Amherst, Massachusetts

DEVIL'S PARK STEW

　2　cups instant rice
　1　package sour cream sauce mix
　3　packages instant mushroom soup mix
　1　package cheese sauce mix
¼　cup dry milk
　3　teaspoons oil *or* margarine
　1　teaspoon salt
　3　cups water

AT HOME:
Package rice and other ingredients in separate plastic bags and
label.

IN CAMP:
Add rice to salted boiling water. Mix in other ingredients until
smooth. Let stand 10 minutes until rice is soft. Serves four.

VARIATION:
Add a can of sardines or herring and heat again before serving.

Dr. Robert F. Cozzens
Arlington, Virginia

RICE AND VEGETABLES

    1 cup quick brown rice
    4 dried mushrooms
    1 package onion soup
    2 tablespoons onion flakes *or* 1 medium onion
    2 tablespoons tomato flakes *or* 1 tomato
    1 tablespoon parsley flakes
    1 clove garlic, minced
    2 tablespoons olive oil
    2 tablespoons wheat germ
    1 teaspoon salt
    2 cups water

AT HOME:
Break mushrooms in pieces and package with soup and vegetable flakes. Wash and package fresh vegetables in a plastic bag with a paper towel to absorb moisture. Package rice separately.

IN CAMP:
Soak dry ingredients in water. Chop fresh vegetables and sauté in olive oil in pot. Add water and other ingredients and bring to a boil. Add rice, bring to a boil again and let simmer covered for 20 minutes. Serves two.

SWEET AND SOUR FRIED RICE

    1 cup instant rice
    3 oz. dried chicken, beef, *or* pork
    1 package sweet and sour sauce mix
    1 package fried rice mix
    2 oz. mixed dried vegetables
    ½ teaspoon Chinese Five Spices
    3 tablespoons soy sauce
    3 cups water

AT HOME:
Package ingredients in separate plastic bags and label.

In camp:

Soak vegetables and meat in 1 cup water. Add rice and fried rice mix to 2 cups boiling water, simmer 5 minutes, and set aside. Add sweet and sour sauce mix, soy sauce, and spices to meat and vegetable mix and heat to boiling. Serve on rice. Serves two.

George M. Epple
Providence, Rhode Island

MACARONI, NOODLES, OTHER PASTAS

In camp:

To cook macaroni, noodles, and other pastas, do not follow regular instructions for large amounts of water for cooking. Add pastas to enough boiling water to which oil, butter, bouillon, and/or seasonings have been added, to permit the pastas to boil freely, covered, until *al dente* (slightly resistant to the bite). Then add any other ingredients and stir. Simmer until meat and vegetables are heated, and serve.

Patsy Stroble
Larchmont, New York

Spaghetti alla Carbonara derives its name from the *Carbonari*, nineteenth-century Italian charcoal sellers and members of a secret political organization.

BACKPACKER'S PASTA ALLA CARBONARA

        ¾ lb. elbow macaroni *or* spaghetti
         4 oz. powdered eggs
        ⅓ cup imitation bacon bits
         2 tablespoons parsley flakes
        ⅓ cup grated Parmesan cheese
         3 teaspoons salt
         3 tablespoons margarine
       4–5 cups water

AT HOME:
Package macaroni and egg in separate plastic bags. Mix other dry ingredients in a third bag.

IN CAMP:
Boil macaroni in salted water until tender. Drain and stir in margarine. Mix egg with cold water into a smooth paste. Mix in grated cheese, bacon, and seasonings. Mix with macaroni until well coated. Heat briefly before serving. Serves four.

Jim Giorgi
Bronx, New York

BEEFARONI

         1 7-oz. package macaroni and cheese
        ½ cup textured vegetable protein (TVP)
         2 tablespoons freeze-dried mushrooms
         1 tablespoon onion flakes
         2 6-oz. cans vegetable *or* tomato juice
        ½ teaspoon salt
        ¼ teaspoon black pepper
         3 cups water

AT HOME:
Package all dry ingredients except macaroni and cheese in a plastic bag and label.

IN CAMP:
Boil macaroni until done. Add TVP, mushrooms and onions, seasonings, and juice. Simmer 10 or 15 minutes, stirring to prevent sticking. Serve topped with powdered cheese. Serves two.

Ronald J. Landis
Oxon Hill, Maryland

CHICKEN SAUCE WITH NOODLES

      2 cups egg noodles
      1 tablespoon dried mushrooms, cut in pieces
      1 3-oz. package Protein-ettes (soy protein)
      2 packages instant chicken soup
      2 teaspoons instant chicken bouillon powder
      1 teaspoon instant minced onion
    ¼ teaspoon pepper

AT HOME:
Package noodles and mushrooms in a plastic bag. Package other ingredients in a second plastic bag, and label both.

IN CAMP:
Boil noodles in a minimum amount of water until done. Add contents of second bag and cook slowly for 5 minutes. Serves three.

Marian Hodesson
Tucson, Arizona

MEXARONI

   1¼ cups Sesame Elbow Macaroni
     1 package French's Enchilada Sauce
    ¼ cup dried mixed vegetables
    ¼ cup powdered milk
    ½ cup grated Parmesan cheese
    ½ teaspoon salt
    ¼ teaspoon cayenne, or more, to taste
    5 cups water

AT HOME:
Mix all ingredients except cheese in a plastic bag and label.

IN CAMP:
Pour mixture into a pot with 5 cups water, stir until well mixed, and bring to a boil. Simmer 15 minutes or until macaroni is done. Mix in cheese, or add to each serving as a topping. Serves four.

Debbie Nicholson
Idaho Springs, Colorado

MIZU TAKI

    12 oz. Japanese noodles (Top Ramen, etc.)
     2 oz. freeze-dried mixed vegetables
     4 packages Chicken Cup-o-Soup mix
  2½ oz. freeze-dried chicken
     4 eggs, hard-boiled
    ½ teaspoon salt
    ¼ teaspoon pepper
     5 cups water

AT HOME:
Package vegetables and soup mix in a plastic bag, with chicken. Package noodles and hard-boiled eggs separately.

IN CAMP:

Add vegetables, soup, and chicken to water, and soak 10 minutes. Bring to a boil, simmer 3 minutes and stir in noodles. Mix in diced eggs. Serves four.

Jack Palmer
San Diego, California

Dried Fruits, Vegetables, & Meats

DRIED PARSLEY AND OTHER HERBS

    2 or 3 bunches parsley
       boiling water

Cut clusters of parsley from the stems and plunge into boiling water for 30 seconds. Drain, spread on wire screen, on oven rack. Set oven at lowest temperature with door ajar until leaves are dry and crisp, 2–3 hours. Store in tins or plastic bags. Keep dry.

> Parsley contains Vitamins A and C. It was used in ancient Greece and Rome to offset the effects of too much wine.

Oregano, rosemary, and other herbs may be placed on a window ledge or other sunny spot and dried by sun and air, in two or three days. Remove dried leaves from stems and store in 35mm. film cans or plastic bags. Keep dry.

APPLESAUCE LEATHER

    8–10 apples, cored and chopped
       1 tablespoon lemon juice
       1 tablespoon honey
      ½ teaspoon nutmeg (optional)
      ½ teaspoon cloves *or* cinammon (optional)
       2 teaspoons ginger root, grated (optional)

AT HOME:
Purée apples in blender with lemon juice and seasonings. Spread a plastic film over baking sheet, overlapping edges. Spread apple-

sauce thinly over plastic. Dry in a 140°F. oven for 12–15 hours, or until dry enough to peel off plastic. Roll into plastic and keep in a cool place until needed.

ON THE TRAIL:
Give each hiker a roll of leather for lunch or snacks.

VARIATION:
Spread 1 can (2 cups) applesauce on film and dry in same manner.

FRUIT LEATHER

Any fruit or berries in season may be made into fruit leather. Peaches, apricots, rhubarb, and persimmons are good choices.

AT HOME:
Wash fruit, pit, or remove seeds and cut out any discolorations, but do not peel. Purée in a blender with about 2 tablespoons water to make 2 cups of fruit purée. Season to taste with lemon juice, spices, and a tablespoon of honey or sugar. Line a 12″ x 17″ cookie sheet with heavy plastic wrap (not foil) fastened with masking tape on the bottom of the pan. Spread purée evenly and dry 6 to 8 hours in hot sun, or overnight in a 150° oven. While still warm, turn out leather, peel off plastic, and lay on a clean sheet of plastic or waxed paper. Roll and store in a dry, cool place.

ON THE TRAIL:
Take along a roll of leather for a snack or lunch.

> *Helene Csvany*
> *Akron, Ohio*

DRIED APPLES

   7 lbs. apples

AT HOME:
Core apples, peel if desired, and slice no thicker than ¼″. Spread

on a cookie or baking sheet and air-dry for several days, turning occasionally, or place in a warm oven (140° to 180°F.) overnight. Seven pounds of fresh apples should make one pound of dried. Peaches and nectarines can also be dried this way.

Ann Kramer
Flagstaff, Arizona

DRIED CRANBERRIES

1 lb. cranberries

AT HOME:
Spread berries on baking sheets and dry in a 140°F. oven for 3–4 hours, or until dry. Makes about 3 ounces. Store in a closed tin in a cool place until needed.

TO USE:
Mix with dried meat as pemmican, or eat with other fruits for lunch or snacks.

SOY NUTS

1–2 lbs. soybeans

AT HOME:
To roast soy nuts, soak the soybeans overnight, or about 12 hours. Drain, spread on an oiled baking sheet, and roast in a 250°F. oven for about 2 hours, or until browned. Stir often to be sure the nuts brown evenly.

TO USE:
Mix with dried fruits and other nuts as trail snacks, or add to soups and stews. Grind the nuts and add to breads, soups, or other foods prepared at home or in camp.

DRIED VEGETABLES

ZUCCHINI CHIPS

AT HOME:
Slice zucchini in rounds ¼″ thin, salt, and lay on a greased baking sheet or screen in a 150°F. oven for 6–8 hours, or until dried. Turn after first 30 minutes to be sure none of the rounds are sticking to the pan. Package for use in lunches, or in soups and stews.

CARROT CHIPS

Prepare in the same way as zucchini. Use in soups and stews.

BEET CHIPS

Cut cooked beets into ¼″ slices and dry in the same way as other vegetables.

YAM CHIPS

Slice raw yams and dry in the same way as other vegetables.

DRIED BEANS OR LENTILS

1 lb. beans (any kind) *or* lentils

AT HOME:
Put beans or lentils in pressure cooker without rack. Cover with water 2 inches above level of beans. Pressure-cook for 30 minutes or as directed by pressure-cooker instructions. Drain well, spread in a single layer on baking sheets, and dry in oven at lowest heat until dry and hard. Ovens vary: it will take 12 hours (overnight) with a gas oven pilot only, or about 6 hours at 140°F., and approximately the same time in an electric oven with its lowest setting. If a home dehydrator is used, follow instructions for drying cooked beans.

FOR THE TRAIL:
Measure desired amount of beans into a plastic bag with onion flakes, tomato flakes, bouillon cubes, bacon bits, or other vegetables and seasonings.

IN CAMP:
Soak the mixture 10 minutes. Bring to a boil and simmer 10 to 15 minutes or until tender.

> *D. Dautremont*
> *Northridge, California*

SWEET PARCHED CORN

AT HOME:
Cut the kernels from fresh garden corn. Let kernels dry overnight in a wide flat pan, then place pan in a medium oven (300°–350°F.) and parch corn until light brown. Sprinkle evenly with 2–3 tablespoonfuls brown sugar. Reheat until the sugar melts. Cool mixture and grind it in a food grinder. Store in a tin or plastic bag in a cool place. A pound of corn reduces to about ½ lb. dried.

ON THE TRAIL:
Eat a tablespoon of the ground corn in the morning, and a tablespoon in the evening. Wash it down with plenty of water. It can be supplemented with wild berries picked on the trail or with a stick of beef jerky. Good food for the survival kit.

VARIATION:
Parch and salt corn as a trail snack.

> *Billy Rosy*
> *Aberdeen, North Carolina*

ROCKHOMINY

AT HOME:
Toast fresh corn kernels on a baking sheet in a 150°F. oven until they are the color of crisp bacon—about 30 minutes. Cool, crush with a hand coffee grinder or a hammer. Make the bits small enough to swallow, but not "dusty." Store in a plastic bag until needed.

ON THE TRAIL:
Eat 3 tablespoonfuls per meal, and swallow with water, for a filling lunch.

IN CAMP:
Cook in boiling salted water—2 cups of water to 1 cup of corn—until done, for a hot, thick mush.

Charles R. Blair

TOMATO CONCENTRATE

1 can (2 cups) tomato sauce

AT HOME:
Simmer sauce until thick, stirring to prevent sticking. Pour thickened sauce on an oiled baking pan and place in a slow oven (300° to 325°F.) to dry. Check often to be sure mixture does not burn. After 2 or 3 hours, the mixture can be cooled and rolled into a ball. Two cups of sauce will reduce to a 2-oz. ball. Wrap in foil or tie in a plastic bag.

IN CAMP:
Dilute the concentrate in 2½ cups of water. Add dried vegetables, rice, and other foods to make a flavorful stew. Simmer until done, about 15 minutes.

Spencer E. Schweinhart
Marlow Heights, Maryland

OVEN-DRIED MEATS

AT HOME:
Cut window screening to fit oven racks, and purchase more racks if you dry more than 2 or 3 lbs. of meat at a time. For an electric oven, set heat at lowest level, around 180°. For gas ovens, use pilot-light heat. Oven temperatures will vary, so drying time will depend on each individual oven.

DEHYDRATED GROUND MEATS

Lean ground beef, chicken, turkey, or ham may be used. Fry meat briefly to remove excess fat and water. Chicken and turkey may be baked or stewed, then ground and dried. Spread ground meat on racks and dry overnight, or until crisp. Usually, 6–8 hours will be enough for partially cooked meats.

Store in plastic bags—1 cup to each bag—and freeze. These meats may be added to stews, casseroles, spaghetti, etc. Allow 2 oz. dried meat per person per serving.

JERKY

Beef, venison, chicken, turkey, or ham may be used. Remove all fat and slice meat thin—¼″–⅛″ slices. The thinner the meat, the faster it dries. Sprinkle with salt, pepper, garlic or other seasonings, as desired. Lay slices of meat on racks and dry overnight (8–10 hours), or as required. Beef and venison take longer than poultry or ham. Meat will reduce to one-quarter or one-fifth of its original weight, depending on fat and water content.

Barbara Schwaiger
La Crescenta, California

DEHYDRATED GROUND BEEF

1 lb. ground beef

AT HOME:
Brown meat and drain fat. Spread on paper towels to remove fat. Next, spread meat on a baking sheet and place in a 150°F. oven overnight, 9–10 hours. The meat will shrink in volume to about one-fourth its original size and weight. Store in a tin or plastic bag in a cool place.

FOR THE TRAIL:
Combine the meat with spaghetti sauce mix, beef gravy, sour cream mix, or cheese, to use with any choice of starch and other vegetables.

IN CAMP:
Cook the rice or noodles in boiling salted water, drain, and add beef and sauce mix and vegetables. Simmer 10 minutes. Serves two or three.

> *Pat Henkel*
> *Browns Mills, New Jersey*

DRIED MEAT, MEATBALLS, AND PATTIES

> 1 lb. ground turkey, chicken, beef, lamb, *or* pork
> 1 teaspoon thyme (for pork sausage—optional for other meats)
> 1 teaspoon sage (for pork sausage)
> 1 teaspoon basil (optional)
> 1 teaspoon black *or* red pepper
> 1 tablespoon salt *or* 1 tablespoon soy sauce

AT HOME:
Mix seasonings with meat and spread the meat on baking sheets about 1/4" thick. Place in a 150°F. oven and dry about 1 hour. Turn, break into bits, and continue drying 4–6 hours until meat is dry and leathery. This will vary with the kind of meat and amount of water in the tissues. The meat reduces to about one-fourth the original weight. Cool, package in plastic bags, and store in refrigerator.

FOR CAMP:
Package 2 oz. per person per serving for soups, stews, or creamed meat dishes.

MEATBALLS

Form ground meat into balls about 1 1/2" in diameter. Place on baking sheet in a 150°F. oven. Turn after 15 minutes, and again after a second 15 minutes, to prevent balls from flattening. Continue to dry for 4–6 hours, until dry. Package for camp in plastic bags and store in refrigerator until needed.

PATTIES

Form ground meat into patties 2–3 oz. each. Lay on a baking sheet and place in a 150°F. oven. Turn after first hour to permit even drying and prevent sticking, particularly for chicken and turkey. Drain extra fat from pork sausage patties. Continue drying for 4–6 hours, or until crisp or leathery. Package the patties in plastic bags and store in refrigerator until needed.

PEMMICAN AND JERKY (CHARQUI)

The original pemmican was prepared by Plains Indians from dried buffalo, elk, or deer, suet, and berries. The meat was dried on a rack in the sun and became what we call jerky, from the Spanish *charqui*. It was pounded into a powder, mixed with suet, or kidney fat; choke-cherries were often mixed with the meat and suet. Called *wasna* by some tribes, the mixture was nutritious and was easily carried in a leather pouch by scouts and hunters who traveled fast and did not spend time cooking on the trail. We know such a mixture as *pemmican*.

Suet—the fat around beef kidneys—may be melted or "rendered" by cutting it into small pieces and leaving it in a 200°F. oven for about 2 hours. Pour off fat as it accumulates; discard remaining tissue. The fat must be kept chilled to prevent its becoming rancid.

CHARQUI CON CHILE (JERKY)

    6–8 lbs. boneless beef (chuck *or* round)
      3 cups chile sauce
      1 tablespoon salt
      1 tablespoon black pepper

AT HOME:
Slice beef into ¼″ thick strips 6″–8″ long. Marinate strips in chile sauce (p. 205) overnight. Drain, sprinkle with salt and pepper on both sides. Spread strips on a rack in a shallow pan and place in a 140°F. oven for 5–6 hours. Leave oven door ajar to permit moisture to escape. *Or,* air-dry for two or more days by hanging strips over double lines of string 2″ apart in a screened area.

Benny Sena, Sr.
Las Animas, Colorado

BEEF JERKY I

  4 lbs. lean beef (flank, rump, brisket *or* round)
1½ tablespoons salt
  1 teaspoon pepper
  2 teaspoons onion powder
  1 teaspoon garlic powder
  1 teaspoon Worcestershire sauce
12 drops Tabasco sauce
  ¼ teaspoon thyme

AT HOME:
Trim fat off meat and slice meat with the grain into narrow strips 6″ long and ¼″ thick. Combine seasonings in enough water to cover meat. Soak meat in mixture overnight in refrigerator. Drain and pat dry with paper towels. Lay strips on drying rack covered with paper towels and cheesecloth. Strips should not overlap. Place in oven at 140°F. and let dry for 4–10 hours, leaving door open for circulation of air. Meat is ready when it turns dark and fibrous, and forms sharp points when bent. Store in plastic bags in freezer until ready for use.

Ruth N. Klippstein
Katherine J. T. Humphrey
Cornell University
Ithaca, New York

BEEF JERKY II

1½ lbs. beef (flank *or* round)
1 teaspoon seasoned salt
1 teaspoon onion powder
½ teaspoon garlic powder
¼ teaspoon pepper
½ cup Worcestershire sauce
½ cup soy sauce

AT HOME:
Remove fat from meat. Cut into ¼" thick slices along grain. Meat is easier to slice if it is partially frozen. Combine remaining ingredients to make a marinade. Marinate meat overnight in refrigerator. Drain. Lay meat strips on oven rack and place foil on bottom rack to catch drippings. Leave door ajar. Set oven at 150° and dry meat for 6 hours. Turn oven off and leave meat to dry for another 6 hours. Store jerky in covered container with holes punched in lid.

Caroline Johnson
Tulsa, Oklahoma

JERKY, HOOPA INDIAN STYLE

10 lbs. venison
¼ cup salt
4 tablespoons black pepper

AT HOME:
Slice venison into ½" thick strips and place in salted water. Bring to a boil, remove from fire, and drain. Pepper on both sides and spread meat on racks. Let dry in 140°F. oven for 12–18 hours. Store in tins, covered, until needed. Makes 2–3 lbs. dried meat.

TURKEY JERKY

3½ lbs. breast meat from 10–12-lb. turkey
3 tablespoons coarse salt

AT HOME:
Skin breast of turkey and remove breast bone with a boning knife.
Place meat in a pan and salt liberally. Let stand for 6–7 hours.
Slice meat into thin lengthwise slices about ¼″ wide. Lay on a
rack and dry in a 150°F. oven for 12 hours. Makes ¾ lb. of jerky.
Package in covered tins or plastic bags and store in refrigerator
until needed.

PEMMICAN

8 oz. dried beef (ground or crushed strips)
4 oz. melted suet (beef kidney fat)
4 oz. cranberries, dried (2 cups)
½ teaspoon salt
¼ teaspoon cayenne
½ cup toasted sunflower seeds
4 tablespoons chia seeds

AT HOME:
Dry cranberries (p. 237) and beef. Break up jerky strips into fine
pieces or crush. Chop suet in pieces and melt in a slow oven
(300° to 325°F.) and mix all ingredients. Place a sheet of foil in a
9″ x 5″ baking pan and pour in the warm mixture. Let harden in
refrigerator. Cut into slices and package in plastic bags. Freeze
until needed.

ON THE TRAIL:
This is best for cold weather; it should be eaten in small quantities
because it is very rich.

VARIATION:
Substitute 1 cup raisins for cranberries and season with ⅛ teaspoon curry powder. Chopped nuts may be added.

EASLEY'S PEMMICAN

  8 oz. beef suet (kidney fat)
  2 2½-oz. jars dried chipped beef
  1 6½-oz. can roasted peanuts
  1 cup raisins

AT HOME:
Chop suet in small pieces and spread in a shallow baking pan, and melt in a 200° oven for about 2 hours. Dry beef for 20 minutes in a 140° oven. Shred beef into small pieces and combine with melted fat and other ingredients. Spread in a ½" thick layer in a shallow pan and refrigerate until hard. Cut into 2" x 3" squares and wrap in plastic or foil. Keeps for months in the freezer, and will keep at least two weeks on the trail.

ON THE TRAIL:
A 3½ ounce bar provides about 440 calories, for lunch or snack.

Bruce W. Easley
Newport News, Virginia

BEEF SALAMI

  5 lbs. ground beef
  2½ teaspoons garlic salt or powder
  2½ teaspoons mustard seed
  1½ teaspoons peppercorns
  2½ teaspoons hickory-smoked salt

AT HOME:
Mix seasonings thoroughly into meat and roll mixture into a ball. Cover and refrigerate overnight. On the second, third, and fourth days, knead well and replace in refrigerator. On the fifth day, divide mixture into ten ½-lb. portions and form each portion into a tightly rolled log about 2" in diameter. Lay the logs on a rack in a shallow pan and dry in a 150°F. oven for 8–10 hours. Remove

logs from oven and cool on paper towels to absorb remaining fat. Roll in plastic wrap or foil and store in freezer until needed.

Seasonings may be varied—more garlic powder and 2 tablespoons oregano leaves or other herbs are good.

Cathie Schafer
Loveland, Colorado

Fish, Poultry, & Meats

OYSTER CHOWDER

    1 can smoked oysters
    1 package instant onion soup
  1½ cups instant potato flakes
    1 package sour cream sauce mix
  1½ tablespoons powdered milk
    3 cups water

AT HOME:
Package soup and potatoes in a plastic bag. Package sour cream sauce and milk in a second plastic bag.

IN CAMP:
Mix oysters, soup, and potato flakes in water and bring to a boil. Simmer 5 minutes. Mix sour cream sauce and milk in enough water to form a thin paste, and add to the soup mixture. Serves two.

Elaine Rowe
Newport, Oregon

SHRIMP LOVE

    1 4½-oz. can shrimp
  1½ cups instant rice
    2 packages instant lobster bisque
    1 tablespoon parsley flakes
    ½ teaspoon salt
    2 cups water

AT HOME:
Package soup, parsley, and rice in one plastic bag.

IN CAMP:
Add soup and rice mixture to boiling salted water and boil 1 minute. Cover and let stand 10 minutes. Add shrimp, cover and let stand 5 minutes longer. Serves two.

VARIATION:
Substitute lobster for shrimp.

> *George Ford*
> *Quakertown, Pennsylvania*

SWEET AND SOUR SHRIMP

>   1 8-oz. can shrimp *or* 4 oz. dried shrimp
>   1 package sweet and sour sauce
>   2 tablespoons green pepper flakes
>   2 tablespoons celery flakes
>   1 tablespoon ginger root, minced
>   1 oz. dried pineapple
>   ¼ teaspoon curry powder
>   1 teaspoon soy sauce
>   2 tablespoons butter
>   3 oz. instant rice
>   3 cups water

AT HOME:
Package all dry sauce ingredients in a plastic bag. Package rice in a second plastic bag. Pour soy sauce into a plastic bottle.

IN CAMP:
Bring 1½ cups water to a boil, add salt, butter, and rice. Boil 1 minute, set aside for 10 minutes. In a second pot, soak sauce ingredients, and dried shrimp if used, in 1½ cups water for 10 minutes. Bring to a boil, add canned shrimp if used, and simmer until sauce is thick and mixture is hot. Serve over rice. Serves two.

CARIBBEAN SHRIMP AND YAM STEW

   8 oz. canned shrimp *or* 4 oz. dried shrimp
  ½ lb. precooked and dried yams
   4 tablespoons onion, minced, *or* 2 tablespoons flakes
   1 tablespoon tomato concentrate *or* flakes
   1 clove garlic, minced
   1 teaspoon dry mustard
   1 tablespoon Worcestershire sauce
   1 tablespoon powdered milk
   1 cup water

AT HOME:

Package dried shrimp, dried yams (p. 238), tomato concentrate
(p. 240) or flakes, and seasonings in a plastic bag. Package milk in
a second bag, and Worcestershire sauce in a small plastic bottle.

IN CAMP:

Soak all dried ingredients in water 15 minutes. Bring to a boil
and simmer 10 minutes. Add milk and heat 5 minutes, but do not
boil. If canned shrimp is used, add with milk and heat slowly.
Serves two.

SEA ISLAND GRITS AU GRATIN

   1 4-oz. can shrimp
  ⅔ cup quick or instant grits
   4 oz. Cheddar cheese, finely chopped
   4 tablespoons butter
  ½ teaspoon salt
  ¼ teaspoon black pepper
 2⅔ cups water

AT HOME:

Package all ingredients in separate plastic bags.

IN CAMP:

Bring water to a boil, add salt and grits. Return to a boil, add cheese and pepper, and stir until cheese melts. Add shrimp, heat about 5 minutes. Top each serving with butter. Serves four.

Stephen Johnson
Atlanta, Georgia

SHRIMP CHOP SUEY

    2 4-oz. cans shrimp
    1 4-oz. can mushrooms
    2 carrots, sliced into strips
    2 cloves garlic, minced
    1 tablespoon soy sauce
    3 tablespoons oil
    3 oz. instant rice
$1\frac{1}{2}$ cups water

AT HOME:
Package rice in a plastic bag. Wash carrots and package in a second bag with a paper towel to absorb moisture.

IN CAMP:
Bring water to a boil, add salt and water from shrimp and mushroom cans. Add rice, boil 1 minute, set aside for 10 minutes. Slice carrots into thin strips, and add with other ingredients to heated oil in frying pan. Stir-fry until vegetables are partially cooked but crisp. Serve over rice. Serves two or three.

Jo Ann Rakus
Rock Island, Illinois

✿ SEAFOOD STROGANOFF

    1 6-oz. can salmon
    1 4-oz. can shrimp *or* 2 oz. dried shrimp
    1 oz. onion flakes
    2 dried mushrooms, broken in bits
    1 package sour cream sauce *or* ½ cup sour cream
    1 tablespoon lime juice
  ½ teaspoon cayenne
  ½ teaspoon salt
    4 oz. spinach noodles
    1 tablespoon oil
    2 cups water

AT HOME:
Package dry ingredients for sauce in a plastic bag. Package noodles in another plastic bag. Pour oil and lime juice into small plastic bottles.

IN CAMP:
Soak dried ingredients in water to cover then bring to a boil. Add salmon and canned shrimp, if used, and heat until mixture thickens. Boil noodles in water with salt and oil until *al dente*—just done. Serve fish mixture over drained noodles. Serves two or three.

✿ SALMON IN HERB BUTTER

    2 salmon steaks, about 1″ thick
    2 oz. butter
    1 clove garlic, minced
    2 green onions, minced
    2 tablespoons parsley
    1 tablespoon tarragon leaves
    1 tablespoon dill weed
    1 lemon, juice and grated rind
    1 teaspoon salt
  ½ teaspoon black pepper

AT HOME:
Package vegetables and dry seasonings in a plastic bag. Put butter, lemon juice and rind in a plastic bottle or jar. Wrap frozen steaks in foil and place in plastic bag.

IN CAMP:
Melt butter and add seasonings. Brush over salmon steaks and cook over hot coals or in a frying pan. When brown on one side, turn and add rest of herb butter to pan or steaks. Cook about 4 minutes on each side. *Do not overcook.* Serves two.

VARIATION:
This recipe may be made with any fish steak or filet.

SALMON RICE POT

> 1 6-oz. can salmon
> 1 package mushroom soup
> 3 tablespoons celery flakes
> 1 tablespoon pepper flakes
> 4 oz. instant *or* quick rice
> 2 cloves garlic, minced
> 1 tablespoon dry mustard
> 3 oz. Cheddar cheese, grated
> 1 teaspoon salt
> 1 teaspoon cayenne
> 3 cups water

AT HOME:
Package soup mix, vegetables, and seasonings in a plastic bag, the rice in a second bag, and the cheese in a third bag.

IN CAMP:
Add soup and seasonings to water and bring to a boil. If instant rice is used, add and boil 1 minute, mix in salmon and cheese, and set aside 10 minutes. If quick rice is used, add to soup and simmer 10 minutes. Mix in salmon, and simmer 5–10 minutes, or until rice is soft. Mix in cheese and let melt. Serves two.

VARIATION:
Smoked salmon is good, too.

✿ TROUT AND HERBS

> 1–2 trout per person
> 1–2 sprigs western pennyroyal

IN CAMP:
Poach trout in a scant covering of water with pennyroyal until just done, not overcooked. Use some of the mint-flavored pennyroyal to make tea. (Pennyroyal, of the family Labatae, is common in the Sierra Nevada of California.)

> *Steve Wolf*
> *Rosemary McKinnon*
> *New Haven, Connecticut*

✿ PINEAPPLE TROUT

> 3–4 trout
> 1 package (1 oz.) freeze-dried pineapple
> 4 oz. instant rice
> 4 tablespoons butter
> ½ teaspoon salt
> 1½ cups water

AT HOME:
Chop pineapple into small pieces and package in plastic bag. Package rice in a second bag. Put butter into plastic screw-top jar.

IN CAMP:
Soak pineapple in water to cover. When soft, place several pieces in the cavity of each trout and sauté in butter until just done. Heat water, with pineapple soaking water, and bring to a boil. Add rice, boil 1 minute and set aside for 10 minutes. Serves two.

✿ TROUT CHOWDER

  2–4 trout, cleaned, boned, and cut into pieces
    1 bacon bar (2 oz.), crumbled
    1 package (6 oz.) hash-brown potatoes
    3 tablespoons onion flakes
  ½ teaspoon salt
  ¼ teaspoon pepper
    3 cups water

AT HOME:
Package vegetables and bacon bar in a plastic bag.

IN CAMP:
Soak vegetables and bacon bar in water 15 minutes. Bring to a boil and cook mixture 15 to 20 minutes. Add trout and cook 5 minutes longer. Serves three.

Jane L. Krampert
Mount Prospect, Illinois

TROUT AND NOODLES

  3–4 trout
    4 dried mushrooms, broken in bits
    1 package Oriental noodles (beef, pork, chicken)
    1 zucchini, chopped finely
    4 oz. Cheddar cheese, grated
    2 tablespoons butter
    2 cups water

AT HOME:
Package ingredients in separate plastic bags.

IN CAMP:
Soak mushrooms 10 minutes in water and add noodles. Boil 5 minutes. Chop zucchini fine and sauté. Sauté trout until barely done. Serve noodles topped with zucchini, deboned trout, and grated cheese. Serves two.

VARIATION:
Add chopped green onions or other crisp, chopped vegetable that does not overwhelm the delicate trout flavor.

Chris Millington
June Lake, California

DEVIL'S THUMB STEW

   1 6-oz. can tuna
   1 package (12 oz.) macaroni and cheese
   1 package vegetable beef soup
  ½ cup instant rice
   4 cups water

AT HOME:
Package all ingredients together except rice.

IN CAMP:
Bring water to a boil, add soup and macaroni mixture. Simmer until macaroni is almost done, about 10 minutes. Add cheese and tuna, and the rice. Bring to a boil and simmer 10 minutes longer. Serves four.

Ed Stahl
Fraser, Colorado

TUNA BULGUR

   1 6½ oz. can tuna, bonito, albacore
 1½ cups bulgur
   1 vegetable bouillon cube
   2 packages mushroom soup
   1 teaspoon onion salt
   1 teaspoon parsley flakes
  ½ teaspoon thyme
  ½ teaspoon basil
   3 cups water

AT HOME:
Mix all ingredients except soup and tuna in a plastic bag.

IN CAMP:
Sauté the bulgur mixture for a few minutes in the oil from the tuna. Add water, bouillon cube, and soup mix. Bring to a boil and simmer about 20 minutes, or until liquid is absorbed. Stir in tuna and heat. Serves four.

Ann Kramer
Flagstaff, Arizona

❃ CHICKEN FLAMENCO

   2 chicken breasts
   2 tablespoons olive oil
  ½ teaspoon salt
   1 teaspoon cayenne
   1 cup eggplant, cut in ½" dice
   2 onions, diced
   2 potatoes, diced
   2 tomatoes, diced
   2 cloves garlic, minced

AT HOME:
Heat oil in frying pan, salt and pepper chicken breasts and brown on both sides. Cook until done, drain, cool, and wrap in foil. Brown eggplant, garlic, onions, potatoes and tomatoes. Simmer, covered, 5 to 10 minutes. Cool, wrap in foil, and freeze both vegetables and chicken.

IN CAMP:
Place thawed vegetables in pot with ½ cup water and top with chicken breasts. Cover, bring to a boil, and simmer until heated. Serves two. A good first night's dinner.

CHICKEN AND STUFFING

    1 small (5-oz.) can boned chicken
   ½ package prepared stuffing with herbs
    4 dried mushrooms, broken in bits
    2 tablespoons onion flakes
    1 tablespoon celery flakes
    2 cups water

AT HOME:
Package stuffing in a plastic bag, and the vegetables together in a second bag.

IN CAMP:
Soak vegetables in water until soft. Bring to a boil, and add chicken, broken into pieces. Add stuffing mix and remove pot from fire. Mix well. Serves two.

VARIATION:
For four to six people, use 2 cans chicken and one bag stuffing. For seven to eight people, use 2 bags stuffing, 4 cups water.

Bob Nass
Colorado Springs, Colorado

GINGER CHICKEN

    1 5-oz. can chicken
    3 oz. instant rice
    2 tablespoons chicken bouillon powder
    2 green onions, minced
    2 tablespoons butter
   ½ teaspoon salt
   ¼ teaspoon black pepper
    2 tablespoons powdered milk
   ¼ cup Madeira
    4 tablespoons crystallized ginger, minced
    2 cups water

AT HOME:
Package rice and bouillon in a plastic bag. Package onions in a second bag and ginger in a third bag. Pour Madeira into a small plastic bottle.

IN CAMP:
Mince green onion. Bring water to a boil, add butter, onions, chicken, rice, and seasonings, except milk, Madeira, and ginger. Simmer 10 minutes. Stir in milk and Madeira, simmer 2 minutes. Serve topped with minced ginger. Serves two.

ORIENTAL CURRIED CHICKEN

    1 5-oz. can boned chicken
    ½ package vegetable soup mix
    1 oz. mixed celery, onion, and pepper flakes
    4 oz. instant rice
    ½ package curry sauce mix *or* 1 tablespoon curry powder
    3 tablespoons powdered milk
    ⅛ teaspoon cayenne
    2 oz. shredded coconut
    2 oz. raisins
    2 cups water

AT HOME:
Package soup mix and vegetables in a plastic bag. Package rice, powdered milk, curry, and cayenne in a second bag, and coconut and raisins in separate bags.

IN CAMP:
Soak vegetables and soup in water. Bring to a boil. Add seasonings, rice, chicken, and simmer 10 minutes. Add milk, simmer 1 minute. Serve topped with coconut and raisins. Serves two.

George M. Epple
Providence, Rhode Island

CHICKEN AND RICE ONE-POT DINNER

  2 cups instant rice
  1 5-oz. can chicken
  2 tablespoons onion flakes
  2 tablespoons celery flakes
  ¼ teaspoon salt
  ¼ teaspoon black pepper
  2 cups water

AT HOME:
Mix all dry ingredients in a plastic bag and label.

IN CAMP:
Add dry ingredients to 2 cups boiling water and simmer 5 minutes.
Stir in chicken and heat 5 minutes longer. Serves two or three.

VARIATIONS:
Add mushrooms or peppers.
  Use fresh green onions or scallions instead of onion flakes.

  J. Stephen Conn
  Spring City, Pennsylvania

CHICKEN AND LENTIL CURRY

  1 6-oz. can chicken *or* 3 oz. dried chicken
  4 oz. precooked dried lentils
  1 tablespoon tomato flakes *or* concentrate
  2 green onions, chopped finely
  2 cloves garlic, minced
  1 tablespoon curry powder
  ¼ teaspoon crushed red pepper
  ½ teaspoon salt
  1 tablespoon oil
  3 cups water

AT HOME:
Package lentils (p. 238), dried chicken (see Oven-Dried Meats, p. 240), tomato flakes or concentrate (p. 240), and seasonings in a plastic bag. Wash and pack onions in a second bag with a paper towel to absorb moisture. Pour oil into plastic bottle.

IN CAMP:
Soak lentils, chicken and tomato in water for 15 minutes. Add oil and minced garlic and bring to a boil. Simmer 15 minutes. Add canned chicken, if used, and heat. Serve topped with chopped green onion. Serves two.

CHICKEN CHOW MEIN

> 1 5-oz. can boned chicken
> 1 package chow mein sauce mix
> 1 6-oz. package Chinese noodles *or* 7 oz. instant rice
> 1 onion, diced
> 2 stalks celery, sliced thinly
> 2 zucchini *or* cucumbers, sliced thinly
> 1 carrot, sliced thinly
> 4 tablespoons oil
> 2 cups water

AT HOME:
Wash, chop and package vegetables in a plastic bag with paper towel to absorb moisture. Package sauce envelope with noodles or rice in a second bag.

IN CAMP:
Sauté vegetables in oil until partially cooked. Add chicken and heat. Mix sauce with 1 cup water and add to vegetables and chicken. Simmer until sauce thickens. In a second pot, bring water to a boil and cook noodles briefly until tender. Or boil rice 1 minute, set aside for 10 minutes to absorb liquid. Serve chow mein mixture over noodles or rice. Serves four.

Jean Simonds
Blacksburg, Virginia

CHICKEN MONTANA

 1 can (5 oz.) boned chicken
 1 package (2 oz.) instant cream of chicken soup
 1 package instant cream of mushroom soup
 1½ cups instant rice
 1½ cups water

AT HOME:
Package soups in one plastic bag and rice in a second bag.

IN CAMP:
Bring water to a boil and add soup mixes. Stir in rice, boil 1 minute, and remove from heat. Let stand 10 minutes, then add chicken and mix well. Serves two.

Libby Medley
Helena, Montana

CREAM OF CHICKEN TOP RAMEN

 1 3-oz. package freeze-dried chicken
 1 3-oz. package chicken-flavored Top Ramen noodles
 1 package instant cream of chicken soup
 1 tablespoon soy sauce
 2 cups water

AT HOME:
Place three packages in one plastic bag. Pour soy sauce into small plastic bottle.

IN CAMP:
Soak chicken in water 10 minutes. Add chicken soup and bring to a boil. Add noodles and cook 1 or 2 minutes. Serve with soy sauce. Serves two.

Gayle Roberts
Lakewood, California

CHICKEN AND DUMPLINGS

    1 6-oz. can chicken
    1 package chicken noodle soup mix
    1 cup Bisquick
    2 tablespoons powdered milk
    3 cups water

AT HOME:
Mix Bisquick and milk and package in a plastic bag.

IN CAMP:
Add soup mix and chicken to boiling water and simmer 5 minutes. Mix Bisquick with ⅓ cup water (in plastic bag) and drop spoonfuls into soup mixture. Simmer 10 minutes uncovered, 10 minutes covered. Serves two.

Mrs. Lee Jemison
Anderson, Indiana

TURKEY PILAF

    6 oz. dried ground turkey
    4 oz. bulgur
    2 tablespoons onion flakes
    2 tablespoons chicken bouillon powder
    ½ teaspoon oregano leaves
    ½ teaspoon mint leaves
    1 tablespoon green and red pepper flakes
    ½ teaspoon salt
    3 cups water

AT HOME:
Package all ingredients but mint leaves in a plastic bag.

IN CAMP:
Soak turkey (p. 242) and other ingredients in water 10 minutes. Bring to a boil, and simmer until done, about 15 minutes. Add mint leaves 5 minutes before done. Serves two.

TURKEY AND MUSHROOM STEW

    8 turkey meatballs
    6 dried mushrooms, broken in bits
    1 package mushroom soup
    4 oz. instant white *or* quick brown rice
  ½ tablespoon tarragon leaves
    3 green onions, minced
    2 tablespoons butter
    3 cups water

AT HOME:
Package turkey meatballs (p. 242) and mushrooms with soup in a plastic bag. Package rice and tarragon in a second bag. Wash onions and package in a plastic bag with a paper towel to absorb moisture.

IN CAMP:
Soak meatballs and mushrooms with soup mix in water. Add minced onion and bring to a boil. Add rice, boil 1 minute and set aside for 10 minutes if instant white rice is used. For quick brown rice, simmer covered 15 or 20 minutes, or until rice is tender. Serves two.

VARIATION:
Noodles (4 oz.) may be substituted for rice. Top mixture with minced parsley.

✿ TURKEY LOAF

    1 lb. ground turkey
  ½ cup breadcrumbs
  ½ cup chopped onion
  ½ cup chopped celery
  ½ cup milk
    2 eggs
    1 tablespoon soy sauce
  ½ teaspoon sage
  ½ teaspoon marjoram
    1 teaspoon black pepper
    2 tablespoons butter
  ½ cup white wine

AT HOME:

Mix all ingredients thoroughly. Pack into a greased 9" x 5" loaf pan and bake in a 350°F. oven for 1 hour. Baste with butter and white wine while cooking. Cool, slice into 8 slices, and wrap each in foil. Freeze until needed.

IN CAMP:

Eat slices of turkey loaf cold for lunch, or serve hot with rice or noodles.

HAM AND RICE SUPREME

> 3 oz. freeze-dried ham *or* ham-flavored
>   textured vegetable protein (TVP)
> 1 cup quick brown rice
> 1 package pea soup mix
> 6 dried mushrooms
> ½ cup dried kale, dried Chinese cabbage,
>   *or* dried spinach *and* celery flakes
> 2 oz. Parmesan *or* Romano cheese, grated
> 1 tablespoon butter
> ½ teaspoon thyme leaves
> 1 teaspoon garlic powder
> ½ teaspoon pepper
> 3 cups water

AT HOME:

Cut mushrooms in pieces and mix together all dried ingredients except cheese. Package in a plastic bag. Grate and package cheese.

IN CAMP:

Pour dried mixture in a pot with water and margarine, bring to a boil. Stir until well mixed. Cover, and simmer 15 minutes, or until rice is done. Top servings with cheese. Serves two or three.

Richard Stolzberg
Fairbanks, Alaska

VIENNA-HAM RICE WITH MUSHROOMS

  4 oz. cooked ham, diced
  1 can Vienna sausages, barbecue style
  2 oz. dried mushrooms, broken in bits
  3 oz. instant white *or* quick brown rice
  1 tablespoon onion flakes
  1 tablespoon pepper flakes
  1 teaspoon thyme leaves
1½ cups water

At home:
Freeze ham and package in a plastic bag. Mix mushrooms and vegetable flakes with rice in a second plastic bag.

In camp:
Add dry ingredients to water and let soak 10 minutes. Bring water to a boil, add rice, thawed diced ham, and sausages. Simmer, covered for 5 minutes for instant white rice, and 15 minutes for quick brown rice. Serves two.

SWEET AND SOUR PORK

1 package freeze-dried pork chops
1 4-oz. package sweet and sour sauce
1 2-oz. package freeze-dried peas
1 4-oz. package dried pineapple
1 8-oz. package Chinese egg noodles
2 tablespoons celery flakes
2 tablespoons green pepper flakes
1 tablespoon soy sauce
1 tablespoon dry mustard
3 cups water

At home:
Chop pineapple into slivers and package with celery and pepper flakes in plastic bag. Mix mustard and soy sauce in a small plastic bottle.

In camp:

Soak meat and vegetables in water to cover. Cut meat into thin strips. Mix sweet and sour sauce with meat, vegetables, and water and bring to a boil. Simmer until the sauce thickens. Soak peas in hot water to cover for 5 minutes, and drain water into pot for noodles. Mix peas with sauce and meat.

Boil 3 cups water in a second pot and add noodles. Cook 5 to 6 minutes and drain. Serve noodles topped with meat and vegetable sauce and garnished with soy and mustard mixture. Serves two.

Dorothy E. Steinberg
Midway, Washington

SAUSAGE WITH LENTILS

    2 4-oz. Polish sausages
    4 oz. precooked dried lentils
    1 teaspoon marjoram leaves
    2 tablespoons parsley flakes
    ½ teaspoon salt
    ¼ teaspoon pepper
    3 cups water

At home:

Package sausages in plastic bag. Package dried lentils (p. 238) with seasonings in a second bag.

In camp:

Soak lentils in water about 15 minutes. Chop sausages into ½″ rounds and add to lentils. Bring to a boil and simmer 15 minutes, or until tender. Serves two.

SAUSAGE RICE

    4 smoked sausages
    1 cup quick brown rice
    2 wedges fresh pineapple
    2 green onions, minced
    1 tablespoon ginger root, minced
    2 cloves garlic, minced
    1 cup water

AT HOME:
Package sausages, rice, pineapple, and vegetables in four separate plastic bags.

IN CAMP:
Add rice to water and bring to a boil. Chop sausages and pineapple into ½″ pieces. Add with minced vegetables to rice. Cover and simmer 10 minutes. Lower heat and simmer 10 minutes longer. Serves two.

SAUSAGE AND SAUERKRAUT

    6 oz. pork sausage patties *or* meatballs
    4 oz. hash-browns *or* potato dice (dried)
    1 cup sauerkraut
    1 apple, chopped
    2 green onions, chopped
    1 teaspoon dill weed *or* 1 teaspoon caraway seed
    1 teaspoon salt
    1 cup water

AT HOME:
Package meat and potatoes in a plastic bag. Wash apple and onions and package with a paper towel to absorb moisture in a second bag. Pack sauerkraut in a screw-top plastic jar, with dill weed.

IN CAMP:
Soak meat and potatoes in water and juice from the sauerkraut

for 15 minutes. Chop apple and onions and add to pot. Simmer 10 minutes, add sauerkraut, and heat for another 10 minutes. Serves two.

✿ GINGER BEEF

> 8 oz. beef sirloin, sliced thinly
> 4 dried mushrooms, broken in bits
> 1 2"-piece ginger root, minced
> 3 green onions, chopped fine
> 2–3 sprigs Chinese parsley (coriander), chopped
> 2 tablespoons vegetable oil
> 1 teaspoon cornstarch
> 2 tablespoons soy sauce

AT HOME:
Wrap sliced beef in foil and freeze, packaged in a plastic bag. Wash vegetables and package in a second bag with a paper towel to absorb moisture. Pour soy and oil into small plastic bottles.

IN CAMP:
Brown thawed beef in oil. Soak mushrooms in water to cover for 10 minutes. Mince ginger root and onions, and add to meat. Simmer 2 or 3 minutes. Mix cornstarch and soy and pour into meat mixture. Simmer 3 or 4 minutes longer and serve over rice or noodles. Top with chopped Chinese parsley. Serves two.

RICE:
Add 3 oz. instant rice to 1½ cups boiling water, and set aside for 10 minutes.

NOODLES:
Boil 1 package (2 oz.) Oriental noodles for 2 or 3 minutes and serve.

✿ MONGOLIAN FIRE-POT

 6–7 oz. beef sirloin, cut in 3" strips ⅛" thick
   4 oz. snow peas, fresh *or* frozen
   2 oz. cellophane noodles (Oriental)
   4 oz. bean sprouts
   4 oz. spinach
   2 green onions, chopped
   4 dried mushrooms, broken in bits
   2 tablespoons chicken bouillon powder
   3 oz. tofu (soybean curd)
   4 tablespoons soy sauce
   1 tablespoon sherry
   1 egg white, well beaten
   1 ½"-piece ginger root, minced
   3 cups water
   2 sets chopsticks

AT HOME:
Package sliced meat in foil and plastic bag and freeze. Wash and package vegetables in separate plastic bags with paper towels to absorb moisture. *Do not wash or crush bean sprouts.*

IN CAMP:
Add bouillon to water and bring to a boil. Prepare a sauce of soy, sherry, and well-beaten egg white with minced ginger root. Lay out meat and vegetables on a plate between the diners. With chopsticks, dip meat and vegetables piece by piece into broth until done, then dip into sauce and eat. When meat and vegetables are eaten, add cellophane noodles to soup and let simmer 3 minutes. Divide between diners, top with bean sprouts, and eat. Serves two.

MEXICAN HASH

        2 oz. freeze-dried beef *or* 4 oz. home-dried
        2 tablespoons onion flakes
        3 oz. hash-brown potatoes (dried)
        1 4-oz. can chopped green chiles
        3 tablespoons Cheddar cheese, grated
        2 tablespoons oil
    ½ teaspoon salt
        1 cup water

AT HOME:
Package beef, onions and potatoes in a plastic bag. Package cheese in a second bag.

IN CAMP:
Soak beef and vegetables in water until soft, about 15 minutes. Pour oil in frying pan, add meat and potatoes and cook until extra water is absorbed. Add chiles and cheese, stir in well, and cook uncovered until mixture browns. Turn and brown on second side. Serves two.

✿ SWEET AND SOUR MEAT LOAF

        2 lbs. ground chuck *or* lamb
        1 8-oz. can tomato sauce
        4 tablespoons brown sugar
    ¼ cup vinegar
        1 egg, beaten
        1 medium onion, chopped
    ¼ cup cracker crumbs
        1 tablespoon dry mustard
    1½ teaspoons soy sauce
        1 teaspoon black pepper

AT HOME:
Mix tomato sauce, sugar, vinegar, and beaten egg. Add other ingredients and combine thoroughly. Bake in a 9″ x 5″ loaf pan

in a 400°F. oven for 45 minutes. Slice in 8 slices, package each in foil, and freeze.

IN CAMP:
Serve for lunch, or heat for dinner with rice or noodles.

VARIATION:
Add diced celery and apple to meat-loaf mixture.

LAMB WITH LENTILS

  4 oz. dried ground lamb
  3 oz. precooked dried lentils
  1 tablespoon tomato flakes *or* concentrate
  1 tablespoon onion flakes
 1/4 teaspoon rosemary, crushed
  1 bay leaf
  1 clove garlic, minced
  2 tablespoons olive oil
 1/2 teaspoon salt
 1/4 teaspoon black pepper
  2 cups water

AT HOME:
Package lamb (p. 242), dried lentils (p. 238), tomato flakes or concentrate (p. 240) in a plastic bag with seasonings. Pour oil in a small plastic bottle.

IN CAMP:
Soak mixture in water for 15 minutes. Add oil, bring to a boil, and simmer 15 minutes or until tender. Remove bay leaf. Serves two.

VARIATION:
Dried ground beef or pork may be substituted for lamb.

✿ PACKAGED DINNER

¼ cup frozen hash-brown potatoes
½ cup frozen mixed vegetables
½ cup frozen ground beef, diced ham, *or* other meat
2 tablespoons chopped onion
1 tablespoon butter or margarine
½ teaspoon salt
¼ teaspoon pepper

AT HOME:
Mix frozen ingredients with onion, seasonings, butter, and place in center of an 18″ square double thickness of heavy-duty foil wrap. Fold and lap edges on two sides, then repeat for second two sides so package is firm and tight. Tie in plastic bag and store in a cool part of backpack. (See "Safety and Perishables," p. 51.)

IN CAMP:
Cook food in package in hot coals 15 minutes. Serves one.

Note: Do not keep longer than first night, except in winter.

Norman L. Petry
Regina, Saskatchewan

Vegetables, Sprouts, & Tofu

BEANS AND LENTILS

Dried beans and lentils have long been staple foods of agricultural man. The pottage Jacob traded his brother Esau in return for Esau's birthright was a lentil stew. Bean or lentil porridge was common fare in Middle Eastern cultures 4,000 years ago. Early European and Asian civilizations relied on these protein-rich legumes, too. In modern times, as meat-eating increased, the reputation of dried beans—red, navy, pinto, lima, soy, and lentils— suffered when they became associated with poverty. Their popularity has been restored somewhat by vegetarians and health-food fans. Precooked and dried, beans and lentils offer ideal fare for backpackers.

BLACK BEANS

    4 oz. precooked dried beans
    1 teaspoon tomato concentrate (optional)
    2 tablespoons onion flakes
    2 tablespoons green pepper flakes
    2 cloves garlic, minced
    1 tablespoon oil
    1 tablespoon vinegar
    3 cups water

AT HOME:
Package precooked dried beans (p. 238) and tomato concentrate (p. 240) with vegetables flakes and garlic. Pour oil and vinegar into a small plastic bottle.

IN CAMP:
Soak beans and vegetables in water 15 minutes. Bring to a boil and simmer 10 to 15 minutes or until tender. Add vinegar and oil just before serving. Serves two.

VARIATION:
Chop 4 Vienna sausages or 1 smoky sausage into beans and heat 5 minutes before serving.

BLACK BEANS AND RICE

> 2 oz. precooked dried black beans
> 2 oz. quick rice
> 2 tablespoons beef *or* chicken bouillon powder
> 2 tablespoons green and red pepper flakes
> 1 tablespoon onion flakes
> 1 teaspoon cayenne
> 1 bay leaf
> 1 teaspoon salt
> 3 cups water
> yoghurt or sour cream (optional)

AT HOME:
Package precooked dried beans (p. 238) with vegetable flakes and seasonings. Package rice in a second plastic bag.

IN CAMP:
Soak beans and vegetables in water 15 minutes. Add bouillon, bring to a boil, and simmer 10 minutes. Add rice, bring to a boil, and simmer 15 minutes, or until rice is tender. Add more boiling water if needed. Serve topped with yoghurt, sour cream, or hot pepper sauce. Serves two.

CASSOULET

> 3 oz. precooked dried white beans
> 2 tablespoons onion flakes
> 2 smoked sausages, cut in 1″ rounds
> 1 oz. dried lamb meatballs
> 1 oz. dried turkey meatballs
> 2 tablespoons parsley flakes
> 2 cloves garlic, minced
> 1 teaspoon dry mustard
> 1 teaspoon black pepper
> 2 tablespoons olive oil
> 3 cups water

AT HOME:

Package precooked dried beans (p. 238) with smoked sausages, dried meatballs (p. 242), and seasonings. Pour olive oil into small plastic bottle.

IN CAMP:

Soak beans and dried meat in water 15 minutes. Slice sausages and mince garlic. Add to beans with oil, and bring to a boil. Let simmer until done, 10 or 15 minutes. Serves two.

KIDNEY BEANS AND SAUSAGES

   3 oz. precooked dried kidney beans
   4 small smoky sausages *or* Vienna sausages
   1 oz. freeze-dried corn
   1 tablespoon onion flakes
   1 tablespoon oregano leaves
   2 cloves garlic, minced
   1 teaspoon cumin
   2 teaspoons chili powder
   1 tablespoon oil
   1 package sour cream sauce
   1 teaspoon salt
   3 cups water
     cornbread (optional)

AT HOME:

Package precooked dried beans (p. 238) with corn, onion flakes, and seasonings. Package sausages and sour cream sauce separately.

IN CAMP:

Soak beans, corn, onion flakes and seasonings in water 15 minutes. Bring to a boil and simmer 10 minutes. Slice sausages, mince garlic, and add to beans. Heat 5–10 minutes. Stir in sour cream sauce and heat. Serve with cornbread. Serves two.

VARIATION:

Use ½ cup yoghurt instead of sour cream sauce.

CHEESE BEANS

    4 oz. precooked dried lima beans
    2 tablespoons beef, chicken, *or* vegetable bouillon powder
    1 4-oz. can chopped green chiles
    1 clove garlic, minced
    ½ teaspoon basil leaves
    ½ teaspoon oregano leaves
    3 oz. Cheddar *or* jack cheese, grated
    1 package sour cream sauce
    1 tablespoon oil
    3 cups water

AT HOME:
Package precooked dried beans (p. 238) with seasonings in a plastic bag. Package cheese and sour cream sauce in separate bags.

IN CAMP:
Soak beans in water 15 minutes. Add bouillon, oil, and chiles, and simmer until beans are soft, about 15 minutes. Add cheese and sour cream sauce. Heat until cheese melts and sour cream is well mixed. Serves two.

DUTCH BEANS

    4 oz. precooked dried pink *or* pinto beans
    2 tablespoons onion flakes
    ½ bacon bar (1 oz.), crumbled
    2 tablespoons oil
    1 small onion, finely chopped
    1 large dill pickle, chopped fine
    3 cups water

AT HOME:
Package precooked dried beans (p. 238) with onion flakes and bacon bar. Package chopped onion and pickle in screw-top plastic jar.

IN CAMP:
Soak beans and onion flakes and bacon bar in water 15 minutes. Bring to a boil, add oil, and simmer until beans are soft, about 10 minutes. Serve topped with onion and pickle. Serves two.

CHUCKWAGON STEW

- 4 oz. precooked dried pinto beans
- 2 slices (3 oz.) salt pork
- 3 oz. freeze-dried *or* home-dried ground beef (optional)
- 2 tablespoons onion flakes
- 2 tablespoons tomato flakes
- 2 tablespoons dry mustard
- 3 cups water

AT HOME:
Cook pork and cut into slivers. Package in a plastic bag with beans (p. 238), onion flakes, tomato flakes, beef (if used), and mustard.

IN CAMP:
Soak all ingredients in water 15 minutes. Bring to a boil and simmer about 15 minutes. Serves two.

REFRIED BEANS

- 4 oz. precooked dried pinto beans
- 1 bacon bar (1 oz.), crumbled (optional)
- 4 oz. Cheddar cheese, grated (optional)
- 2 tablespoons oil
- 2 cups water

AT HOME:
Package precooked dried beans (p. 238) in a plastic bag. Package cheese and bacon bar in separate plastic bags.

IN CAMP:
Soak beans in water 15 minutes. Bring to a boil and simmer until

tender. Turn beans into a frying pan with heated oil and stir, mashing with a fork or wooden spoon. Stir in bacon bar and grated cheese. Serves two.

VARIATION:
Serve wrapped in a Tortilla (p. 96).

> *Mark Adams*
> *Grove City, Ohio*

LENTILS WITH GREENS

> 4 oz. precooked dried lentils
> 1 stalk celery, chopped
> 1 small zucchini, sliced thinly
> 2 green onions, minced
> 1 clove garlic, minced
> 2 tablespoons butter
> ½ teaspoon salt
> ¼ teaspoon black pepper
> 3 cups water

AT HOME:
Package precooked dried lentils (p. 238) in a plastic bag. Wash vegetables and package in a second bag with a paper towel to absorb moisture. Put butter in a screw-top plastic jar.

IN CAMP:
Soak lentils in water 15 minutes. Bring to a boil and simmer 5 minutes. Chop vegetables and add to lentils. Simmer 5 minutes longer. Vegetables should remain crisp. Serves two.

VARIATION:
Top lentils with ½ cup yoghurt.

❁ SPICED LENTILS

4 oz. precooked dried lentils
1 teaspoon red peppers, crushed
1 tablespoon onion flakes
1 tablespoon ginger root, peeled and minced
2 cloves garlic, minced
¼ teaspoon turmeric
2 teaspoons coriander
½ cup yoghurt or sour cream
½ teaspoon salt
3 cups water

AT HOME:
Package dried lentils (p. 238) with vegetable flakes and seasonings in a plastic bag. Package yoghurt or sour cream in a screw-top plastic jar.

IN CAMP:
Soak lentils and seasonings 15 minutes. Mince ginger root and garlic and add to lentils. Bring to a boil and simmer 15 minutes. Top with yoghurt or sour cream. Serves two.

VARIATION:
Add 1–2 tablespoons bacon bits while mixture is cooking.

LENTIL STEW

4 oz. precooked dried lentils
4 tablespoons sesame seeds
2 tablespoons pumpkin *or* sunflower seeds
2 tablespoons dried potato dice *or* flakes
2 tablespoons onion flakes
4 tablespoons textured vegetable protein (TVP)
2 tablespoons powdered milk
1 teaspoon sea salt
1 bay leaf
3 cups water

AT HOME:
Package dried lentils (p. 238) with other ingredients in a plastic bag.

IN CAMP:
Soak ingredients in water for 15 minutes. Bring to a boil and simmer until tender. Serves two.

James R. Palmieri
Ames, Iowa

SPICY LENTILS ON TORTILLAS

    3 oz. precooked dried lentils
    1 oz. short-grain brown rice
    1 tablespoon sesame seeds
    ⅛ teaspoon cumin (comino)
    ⅛ teaspoon curry powder
    ⅛ teaspoon cayenne
    ¼ teaspoon salt
    2 cups water

AT HOME:
Package dried lentils (p. 238) with rice, seeds, and seasonings in a plastic bag. Package flour for Tortillas (p. 96) in a second plastic bag. Pour oil into a small plastic bottle.

IN CAMP:
Add lentil and rice mixture to water and soak 15 minutes. Bring to a boil and simmer until rice and lentils are soft and water is absorbed. Serve on tortillas.

Linnane Blake
Gardner, Colorado

MEATLESS GOULASH

½ cup dried lentils
½ cup split peas
½ cup soy granules
2 cups bulgur, *or* brown buckwheat groats
5 tablespoons brewer's yeast
5 tablespoons powdered milk
2 tablespoons oatmeal, uncooked

AT HOME:
Put lentils and split peas in a blender and grind into meal. Combine with remaining ingredients. Store in a covered tin. Package in plastic bag for camp.

IN CAMP:
To prepare, add ⅔ cup (10 tablespoons) of mixture to 1½ cups salted water. Bring to a boil, stirring occasionally. Simmer 5 to 10 minutes, or until water is absorbed. Serves one or two.

Gerald Salamano
Atlantic City, New Jersey

GREEN BEANS

1 oz. green beans, freeze-dried
1 tablespoon olive oil
1 tablespoon lemon juice
1 clove garlic, minced
1 tablespoon slivered almonds

AT HOME:
Package ingredients separately in plastic bags and bottles.

IN CAMP:
Reconstitute beans in just enough water to cover. Bring to a boil, cook briefly. Drain (using the water for any soup that may be cooking), and add almonds, garlic, oil, and lemon juice. Serve hot or cold. Serves two.

VARIATION:
Add sliced mushrooms, scallions, dill weed, and dress with oil and vinegar. Rosemary and mint leaves are also good seasonings.

CARROTS COOKED WITH MARMALADE

 2 carrots
 1 tablespoon butter
 1 tablespoon orange or ginger marmalade
 ⅛ teaspoon salt

AT HOME:
Wash carrots and package in plastic bag. Package butter and marmalade in plastic bottle.

IN CAMP:
Slice carrots into thin rounds and simmer in water to cover until just barely done. Drain water into any soup that is cooking, and dress the carrots with the butter and marmalade mixture. Let stand a minute or two until butter is melted and serve. Serves two.

VARIATION:
Add fresh mint leaves, dill weed, chives, parsley, nutmeg, or poppy seeds to cooked, buttered carrots.

CARROT SALAD

 2 carrots
 2 oz. raisins *or* dates, chopped
 2 tablespoons nuts *or* seeds
 1 teaspoon ginger root, minced
 ¼ cup pineapple juice

AT HOME:
Package fruit, nuts, and ginger root in a plastic bag. Wash carrots and package in a plastic bag. Put pineapple juice in a plastic bottle.

IN CAMP:
Chop carrots fine and mix in other ingredients. Serves two.

CUCUMBER FETA SALAD

2 cucumbers
3 oz. feta cheese
2 tablespoons oil
1 tablespoon lemon juice
1 tablespoon mint leaves

AT HOME:
Package ingredients in separate plastic bags. Pour oil and lemon juice into a small plastic bottle.

IN CAMP:
Slice cucumbers, crumble cheese, and dress with oil and lemon. Top with mint leaves. Serves two.

FRIED EGGPLANT

1 eggplant
2 tablespoons soy sauce
1 egg, beaten
2 tablespoons wheat germ
3 tablespoons Romano cheese, grated
2 tablespoons olive oil

AT HOME:
Package ingredients separately in plastic bags, egg container, or plastic bottles suitable for travel.

IN CAMP:
Peel and slice eggplant in ½″ slices across. Marinate in soy sauce 15 minutes. Dip in beaten egg and then in wheat germ and cheese. Brown on each side in olive oil. Serves two.

GREEN PEAS

> 1 oz. green peas, freeze-dried
> 2 green onions
> 1 water chestnut
> 1 teaspoon savory leaves

AT HOME:
Package peas in one plastic bag, and the onions and water chestnut in another bag. Package savory in a 35mm. film can.

IN CAMP:
Reconstitute peas in just enough water to cover. Heat with chopped onions, sliced water chestnut, and the savory leaves. Serves two.

VARIATION:
Serve peas cold with sour cream, dill weed, and chives, with a dash of curry powder.

✿ GREEK VEGETABLES

> 1½ cups raw fresh or frozen vegetables (asparagus, artichoke hearts, green beans, Brussels sprouts, broccoli, cauliflower, carrots, mushrooms, zucchini, etc.)
> 3 tablespoons olive oil
> 3 tablespoons wine vinegar *or* lemon juice
> ½ teaspoon salt
> 1 teaspoon ground coriander
> 1 bay leaf
> 1 clove garlic, minced—or more, if desired
> ½ teaspoon black pepper
> 2 cups water

AT HOME:
Wash, dry, and package fresh vegetables in plastic bags. Place frozen vegetables in plastic bags. Package liquids in plastic bottles.

IN CAMP:
Add vinegar and oil to water and bring to a boil. Add vegetables and seasonings, cook uncovered until all are tender-crisp—only a few minutes. Drain, let cool, and serve as a salad. Serves two.

SUKIYAKI SALAD

2–3 spinach leaves, coarsely torn
  2 Chinese cabbage leaves, coarsely chopped
 ¼ cup bean sprouts
  1 stalk celery, sliced diagonally
2–3 water chestnuts, sliced thinly
  2 raw mushrooms, sliced lengthwise
  1 small green pepper, sliced thinly lengthwise
1–2 sprigs watercress *or* Chinese parsley (coriander leaves)
1–2 cloves garlic, minced
  2 tablespoons soy sauce
 ¼ cup olive oil

AT HOME:
Wash vegetables—except bean sprouts—and package with paper towels in plastic bags. The towels absorb moisture and help keep vegetables cool and fresh. Mix liquids and pour into a plastic bottle, with garlic.

IN CAMP:
Prepare vegetables and mix in a bowl. Dress with oil and soy dressing. Serves two.

HOT MUSTARD GREENS

  1 lb. mustard greens
 ¼ bacon bar (½ oz.)
  1 onion, minced
  2 bouillon cubes, any kind
  1 clove garlic, minced
  1 teaspoon salt
 ⅛ teaspoon cayenne

AT HOME:

Wash greens and remove stems. Drain, wrap in paper towel and tie in a plastic bag. Pack other ingredients in a second bag.

IN CAMP:

Chop greens coarsely, put in pot with ½ cup water and other ingredients. Cook over low or medium heat until greens are done, about 15 minutes. Mustard greens take longer than other greens. Serves two.

VARIATIONS:

Use spinach or chard, or other greens in season, but cook only half as long.

Serve greens hot with oil and lemon juice, chopped green onions, or with oil and tarragon vinegar, caraway, poppy, or sesame seeds.

SPINACH SALAD

    1 bunch spinach
    2 oz. feta cheese, crumbled
   10 black olives, pitted
    2 tablespoons olive oil
    1 lemon, juice and rind

AT HOME:

Wash spinach, drain, and package in plastic bag with a paper towel to absorb moisture and keep spinach fresh. Package cheese and olives in separate bags, and the olive oil in a small plastic bottle.

IN CAMP:

Tear spinach leaves into bite-sized pieces. Add crumbled feta cheese and olives, and ¼ teaspoon grated lemon rind. Dress with olive oil and juice of the lemon. Serves two.

YAMS OR SWEET POTATOES

    1 medium yam *or* sweet potato per person
    2 tablespoons butter
  ¼ teaspoon nutmeg
  ⅛ teaspoon ground coriander seed
  ½ teaspoon salt
      oil for frying

AT HOME:
Wash and package yams or sweet potatoes in plastic bag.

IN CAMP:
Bake or boil the yams or sweet potatoes. Do not add sugar; they are sweet enough without it. To fry: peel and slice thin. Salt the slices, let stand for 10 minutes, fry in hot oil, and drain. Sprinkle with nutmeg and coriander. Makes crispy chips that may be eaten for lunch or snacks.

SPROUTS

Fresh greens with the vitamins and enzymes necessary for balanced nutrition are an important addition to the baked and dried foods that make up the backpacking menu. Sprouts are the perfect trail vegetable. There is virtually no extra weight, and growing the sprouts on the trail is easy—even where water is scarce. Beans and most seeds are available in grocery stores or health-food stores. Seeds for sprouting may be obtained from at least one commercial supplier who sells ready-prepared packages of sprouts to grow on the trail. (See Suppliers, p. 22.) Here are some seeds that make good sprouts:

	Growing Time	Yield
Alfalfa seed	3–5 days	1 tablespoon = 4 cups
Chia seed	4–6 days	1 tablespoon = 2 cups
Fenugreek seed	4–6 days	1 tablespoon = 2 cups
Mustard seed	5–6 days	1 tablespoon = 2 cups
Radish seed	2–5 days	1 tablespoon = 2 cups
Lentils	2–4 days	1 tablespoon = 6 cups
Mung beans	1–5 days	1 cup = 5–8 cups
Rye	2 days	1 cup = 4 cups
Wheat	2 days	1 cup = 4 cups

AT HOME:

Most seeds may be sprouted in a quart jar covered with a screen, or in a cheesecloth bag inside a plastic bag. Choose seeds and place in the chosen container.

ON THE TRAIL:

Cover seeds with water overnight. In the morning, drain, and rinse with water two or three times a day until the sprouts have developed. Keep them in a dark place and don't let them become dry.

IN CAMP:

Eat sprouts in sandwiches, salads, soups, and stews.

TOFU

Developed in China over 2,000 years ago, the soybean curd (tofu) serves as the cheese of the Orient and is East Asia's most important soybean food.

The blocks of curd in sealed plastic tubs may be obtained in Oriental markets, natural-food stores, and some supermarkets in West Coast cities, Salt Lake City, Chicago, Boston, New York, and other locations. There is also a dried form which can be made into a curd by adding water to the tofu powder, cooking it briefly, and letting it cool. This is very easy to prepare on the trail.

Tofu in fresh curd (pudding) form will keep for several days without refrigeration, but it will keep longer if it is deep-fried at home. Three types of deep-fried tofu are:

Thick Agé (ag-gay), 5¼ oz.;

Ganmo patties, 3½ oz. each;

Agé pouches, 1 oz. each. The pouches may be filled with grains, raw vegetables, or other stuffing.

Tofu or Agé may be eaten as a substitute for meat or cheese; it provides from 10 to 18 percent protein by weight. Tofu is a complete protein. The soybean is the only legume that contains all 8 essential amino acids.

✿ CRISP DEEP-FRIED TOFU

4–5 oz. Thick Agé or Ganmo
1–2 teaspoons soy sauce
1 tablespoon leeks, sliced thin, grated ginger root,
      minced garlic, *or* other vegetable

AT HOME:
Wash and package vegetables in plastic bag with paper towel to absorb moisture. Package Agé or Ganmo in screw-top plastic container.

In camp:
Cut tofu into bite-sized pieces and serve topped with soy and vegetables. Serves one.

Variation:
Serve topped with maple syrup or honey.

✿ SAUTÉED CARROTS WITH AGÉ

    3 oz. Agé, Ganmo, or Thick Agé
    1 carrot, cut in matchsticks *or* rounds
    1 tablespoon oil
    3½ teaspoons soy sauce
    3 tablespoons toasted wheat germ
    3 tablespoons sunflower seeds *or* almonds

At home:
Wash carrot and package in plastic bag with paper towel to absorb moisture. Package wheat germ and seeds or nuts in a second plastic bag. Package tofu in screw-top plastic container.

In camp:
Heat skillet and coat with oil. Slice carrot and sauté briefly. Add soy, simmer 4 or 5 minutes. Mix in wheat germ or nuts, and serve on tofu. Serve hot or cold. Serves two.

Variation:
Yams may be used instead of carrots. Slice thin and sauté.

❁ CURRIED BUCKWHEAT NOODLES WITH AGÉ

    10 oz. Thick Agé cut in 1″ squares
     2 tablespoons oil
     1 carrot, sliced into thin rounds
     1 onion, thinly sliced
    ⅓ cup raisins
    ½ apple, diced
  1½ teaspoons curry powder
     2 teaspoons soy sauce
    ¼ teaspoon black pepper
    ¼ cup water
     5 oz. buckwheat noodles

At home:
Wash fruit and vegetables and package in plastic bag with a paper towel to absorb moisture. Package other ingredients in separate plastic bags, and the tofu in a screw-top plastic continer.

In camp:
Heat oil in skillet, add sliced carrots and cook 2 minutes. Add sliced onions and cook 2 minutes. Add raisins and diced apple and cook 3 minutes. Stir in water, seasonings, and Agé. Reduce heat and cook 3 minutes. Boil noodles in salted water and drain. Stir into Agé mixture and serve hot or cold, topped with roasted soybeans, peanuts, grated cheese, or chutney. Serves two or three.

❁ THICK AGÉ WITH STEAK SAUCE

     5 oz. Thick Agé or Ganmo
  1½ tablespoons butter
     2 tablespoons green onions, finely chopped
     2 tablespoons ketchup
     5 tablespoons teriyaki sauce
     1 teaspoon mustard
    ¼ teaspoon black pepper

AT HOME:

Wash and package green onions in plastic bag with paper towel to absorb moisture. Package tofu in screw-top plastic container. Mix seasonings in small plastic bottle.

IN CAMP:

Cut Agé into 1″ cubes. Melt butter in a skillet, add onions and sauté. Stir in other seasonings and simmer 1 minute. Serve hot or cold Agé in bowls topped with the sauce. Serves two.

✿ TOFU MEAT LOAF

1½ lbs. ground beef chuck
½ lb. tofu
3 tablespoons fine dry breadcrumbs
1 onion, chopped fine
2 cloves garlic, minced
1 egg
2 tablespoons dry mustard
¼ cup chili sauce
1 teaspoon salt

AT HOME:

Mix together all ingredients and pour into a 9″ x 5″ loaf pan. Bake in a 350°F. oven for 1 hour. Let cool, slice, and package in foil. Store in refrigerator or freezer until needed. Makes eight servings.

IN CAMP:

Serve slices of meat loaf cold for lunch, or heated in foil for dinner, with rice or noodles.

Foods to Make Ahead

BEVERAGES

Barley "Coffee"
Fruit Tea

EGGS

Eggs, Deviled
Egg Salad

CHEESE AND YOGHURT

Yoghurt
Roxanne's Yoghurt
Cheese Balls
Cheese Rolls
Verde Spread

FRIED BREADS, SANDWICHES, AND OTHER FILLED BREADS

Whole Wheat Tortillas
Enchiladas
Pizza Crust
Sandwiches and Sandwich Spreads
Chopped Chicken Livers
Sausage and Pineapple Spread
Tuna Spread
Tofu Spread
Sushi

CRACKERS, FLAT BREADS, AND MUFFINS

Cheese and Dill Crackers
Cobblestone Crackers

Crackers, Flat Breads, and Muffins (continued)

Graham Crackers
Packer's Crackers
Whole Wheat Crackers
Rye Crackers
Rye Pretzels
Roman Rusk
Flat Bread
Molasses Hardtack
Hudson Bay Bread
Logan Bread
Logan Bread, Laura's Way
Oatcakes
Trail Bread
Trail Bread, Greg's Way
White Mountain Survival Bread
Bran Muffins
Carrot Bran Muffins
Fresno Bran Muffins
Millet Apple Muffins
Rice and Raisin Muffins
Soy Muffins
Wheat Berry Muffins

YEAST BREADS, FRUIT BREADS, AND CAKES

Arab Bread (Pita)
Sourdough Starter
Bagels
Bagels, Paul's Way
Bob's Bagels
Raised Oven Donuts
English Muffins
Oat and Fig Bread
Orange Rye Bread
Seven-Grain Bread
Wheat Germ Yoghurt Bread
Apricot Nut Bread
Carrot Fruit Bread
Spicy Fig Loaf

Yeast Breads, Fruit Breads, and Cakes (continued)

Granola Bread
Greg's Everlasting Bread
Honey Quick Bread
Oatmeal Raisin Bread
Orange Fig Bread
Peach Nut Bread
Persimmon Bread
Pumpkin Bread
Walnut Vegetable Bread
Zucchini Bread
Applesauce Cake
Banana Spice Cake
Butter Pound Cake
Boiled Fruitcake
Fruitcake I
Fruitcake II
Mincemeat Cake
Gingerbread

COOKIES, CANDIES, TRAIL SNACKS, AND PUDDINGS

Backpacking Bars
Backpack Snack Bars
Banana Oat Energy Bars
Mincemeat Bars
Mountain Bars
Trail Munchies
Carob Chip Cookies
Carob Nut Cookies
Cannonballs (Hockey Pucks)
Gingersnaps
Ginger-Currant Cookies
Peanut Cookies
Pumpkin Cookies
Raisin Safari Cookies
Aplets
Carob Candy
Carob Fudge
Chocolate Bombers

Cookies, Candies, Trail Snacks, and Puddings (continued)

Wheat Germ Brownies
Fudge Scotch Squares
Munchy Cubes
Coffee Nuggets
Candied Citrus Peel
Fruit Balls
Mediterranean Fruit Balls
Pemmican Fruit Bars
Seed Squares
Backpacker's Delight
Crunch Balls
Grunch
Peanut Butter Balls
Peanut Butter Squares
Peanut Butter Fudge
Peanut Polka Dotties
Hiker's Delight
Fruit and Seed Trail Mix
Trail Snacks
Eddy Gorp
Kaibab Gorp

Soups and Sauces

Chile Sauce for Charqui con Chile
Pesto
Sour Cream Substitute
Tartar Sauce

Cereals, Grains, and Pastas

Maryland Scrapple
Camp Cereal
Easy Granola
Granola
Sun Cloud Granola

DRIED FRUITS, VEGETABLES, AND MEATS

Dried Parsley and Other Herbs
Applesauce Leather
Fruit Leather
Dried Apples
Dried Cranberries
Soy Nuts
Dried Vegetables
Dried Beans or Lentils
Sweet Parched Corn
Rockhominy
Tomato Concentrate
Oven-Dried Meats
Dehydrated Ground Beef
Dried Meat, Meatballs, and Patties
Charqui con Chile (Jerky)
Beef Jerky I
Beef Jerky II
Jerky, Hoopa Indian Style
Turkey Jerky
Pemmican
Easley's Pemmican
Beef Salami

FISH, POULTRY, AND MEATS

Chicken Flamenco
Turkey Loaf
Sweet and Sour Meat Loaf
Packaged Dinner

VEGETABLES, SPROUTS, AND TOFU

Tofu Meat Loaf

Bibliography

Ashley, Richard, and Duggal, Heidi, *Dictionary of Nutrition,* Kangaroo Pocket Books, New York (Simon & Schuster), 1975.

Center for Science in Public Interest, *Chemical Cuisine,* Washington, D.C., 1977.

Dell Publishing Co., Inc., *The Metric Book,* New York, 1976.

Nadja, *The Arabic Cookbook,* California, 1968.

Nemiro, Beverly A., and Hamilton, Donna M., *The High Altitude Cookbook,* New York, 1969.

Shurtleff, William, and Aoyagi, Akiko, *The Book of Tofu,* Massachusetts (Autumn Press), 1975.

Sunset Magazine, California (Lane Publishing Company), February 1974.

Tannahill, Reahy, *Food in History,* New York (Stein & Day), 1973.

U.S. Department of Agriculture, *Nutrition Labeling,* Agricultural Information Bulletin No. 382, 1975.

Index

When the symbol ❀ appears with a recipe in this book, it indicates that the recipe contains perishable ingredients that require special handling for backpacking; consult "Safety and Perishables" on page 51.